AUCTION SUCCESS
An Agents Guide

TOP 10 TIPS
TO SUCCESSFULLY
LIST
PROPERTIES
FOR
AUCTION

PROPERTY SUCCESS SERIES

AUCTION SUCCESS:
TOP 10 TIPS
to SUCCESSFULLY
LIST
properties
for AUCTION

Property Success is a new book series teaching Australians how to buy & sell property at Auction.

This edition is to teach AGENTS how to successfully LIST properties for auction with confidence.

By the end of this book I hope to have convinced you that an Auction Listing is *BY FAR* the *BEST* listing in your portfolio!

I want to encourage you to get out of your comfort zone, dismiss all your fears and *LIST AUCTIONS!*

Author: Lawrance, Maria, author.

Title: Listing @ auction; agent's auction guide; : top 10 tips to successfully list property for auction / Maria Lawrance.

Series: Property success series : auction success ; no 3.
Subjects: Real estate listings--Australia.
Real property auctions--Australia.
Real property--Marketing--Australia.
Real property--Valuation--Australia.
House selling--Australia.

Dewey Number: 333.33220994

ISBN: 9780992416577 (paperback)

CONTENTS

INTRODUCTION

You've chosen this profession because you've heard that you can earn *BIG MONEY*, but you haven't seen any of that yet! You know there are others in your profession out there that are taking home six figures *EVERY YEAR*, but you're not one of them! How come? You work hard, you put the hours in, but somehow, it just doesn't seem to come together for you!

Let me let you into a little secret: if you don't start listing Auctions and marketing Auctions, you will forever be an "also ran" sales agent! Why? Well not only does this system help you to *WORK SMARTER NOT HARDER* it also *SKILLS* you up, *DEADLINES* you and most importantly *IT MAKES YOU MORE ACCOUNTABLE* to your clients than ever before! Because, my friend, if you want to earn big dollars then you have to take more responsibility for your *ACTIONS* and your *COMMITMENT* to this incredible profession!

But the best side of listing auctions is simply this system helps to promote *YOU* in your local community! And when you conduct auctions, whether on site or in rooms, you are inviting the Public to come into *YOUR ZONE* and check you out as an agent! Perform well and the listings will flow through your doors – but be warned! Half-hearted performances will also show you up to the Public!

An Auction Listing is your opportunity to take your office out into the street – no other method of selling is quite like this and I've tried them all. It's an opportunity to

meet the neighbours to the property you've just listed (and let's face it, how many times do you get a listing and then see a domino effect of other houses surrounding your one suddenly have a sales board planted in their yard?), it gives you an opportunity to invite other potential owners to come and see how you work,
and there is a greater chance that complete strangers will come along because they too are thinking of selling!

By the end of this book I hope to have convinced you that an Auction Listing is **BY FAR** the **BEST** listing in your portfolio! I want to encourage you to get out of your comfort zone, dismiss all your fears and **LIST AUCTIONS!**

Last year I handled 22 Auction listings. 1 didn't sell all of them – one owner changed his mind about selling and withdrew the property from the market. For the other 21 Auction listings that I did sell, I collectively got $1,118,000 **OVER** the reserve price for my vendors! That was an average of **$50,000+ OVER THE RESERVE PRICE** per property! How do you think that sounds on my resume when I am out looking for new stock?

So read on my fellow colleagues and let's see if we can turn you into a **CHAMPION SALESPERSON!**

Chapter 1:
What kind of Agent are YOU?

It's pretty obvious that in any industry there are Experts, Adequates and Also-Rans, and it is more pronounced in our Industry than any other. Why? Because we only get **PAID** for **WHAT WE DO** as opposed to what title we hold. I've always believed in the honour of this profession because of this. When a person is paid an hourly rate or a monthly salary for the title they bear then whether they are the best or the worst in their profession their income really doesn't change. Not so with we agents! We, here in Australia, may have a "cushion" income that is an Industry standard weekly wage which is usually then debited against the monthly commission we generate, but most first class performers work on a Commission Only basis to ensure a higher percentage cut of the commission earned by them for their office. To do this in New South Wales you must hold a Real Estate Licence rather than be just a Certificate holder. And seriously, if you are looking at Real Estate as a long term career then you really should be studying to become a Licensed Real Estate Agent rather than just a Certificate holder. However, it is not mandatory, and you can still earn a pretty massive income even as a Certificate holder *IF YOU WORK THE RIGHT WAY.*

So what are the points of difference between the Experts, Adequates and Also-Rans? Most obviously is experience, of course, and skill levels but most important is **ATTITUDE!** I already know you have a good attitude to your career because you are reading this book, which tells me you are willing to learn. Whether this book teaches you anything remains to be seen, and that's my responsibility, but you have picked it up and you are reading it! Good start!

So, where are you in your career today? Are you within your first year or are you longer term that really wants to earn more money? Most importantly, what do you consider to be **BIG MONEY?** To some $80,000 pa sounds good, to others of us there has to be at least five zeros in it! Where do you stand in your thinking? This is crucial! You will only **GET** what you **EXPECT!** And what I have found is that if I break down big money into everyday tasks then my belief in this being doable increases exponentially, giving me a greater chance of achieving these financial goals. More about that later.

I have always used the analogy of comparing us to wood workers, which then falls into basically three types: Tradesman/Handyman, Carpenters and Cabinet Makers. When you read the following work out for yourself which category do you fit into right now?

Tradesman/Handyman

These are fairly competent wood workers with some basic knowledge and skill. They can get the job done, albeit roughly, and they are fairly cheap. They look at their work simply as a job and they are only doing it to earn a living. The quicker they get paid the better, so they won't waste time on finesse, but rather they like to be in and out quickly. Their income is based on volume of turnover and their mantra is probably "near enough is good enough, what do you expect for this kind of money?"

Carpenters

These workers are more skilled than the Tradesman/Handyman, they are working with wood every day. They are usually a little more expensive than a Tradesman/Handyman and they job they do is above average, moderately expensive and adequate. Again, they tend to focus on quantity rather than quality, but they do take pride in the end product.

Cabinet Makers

These wood workers know every tool in their kit and know when to use them appropriately. They know their wood. They know every knot, every twist and every possibility of what that wood can achieve. They love their work and every piece they turn out is done with a level of care and concern that has taken years of dedicated training to achieve. They are expensive, but the quality of their work is unsurpassed.

The difference between these three types of workers is yes, skill, but more importantly **THEIR ATTITUDE** to their job, because it was their attitude that prompted them to skill up and keep skilling up. Everyone starts as an Also-Ran in any profession, but in our Industry there are some salespeople that take off really quickly simply because they are so willing to do whatever it takes to gain expertise. And part of that expertise is knowing all there is to know about the different methods of selling so that when you are at a Market Appraisal, you are absolutely certain of the best advise you can give the client.

I mentioned earlier that if you want to increase your income you need to break everything down into doable tasks so that your belief in earning big money increases. This will then give you a daily/weekly/monthly plan to keep you on track. So if you have been in the industry for over a year you need to go back through all your statistics and work out:

a) How much you earned that year – gross figure
b) How many properties did you sell to achieve that income
c) How many of your listings sold
d) What was your average commission per property

e) How many Market Appraisals you did to get those listings.

For example:

If you earned $100,000 for that year and you are on a 35%/65% split with your office, you had to have brought in $288,000 (approximately) in gross commission to achieve this. If your average commission is $8,000 per property you will have sold 36 properties for the year (at full commission) to achieve this amount. If you have an 85% List to Sell ratio, you will have needed to list 42 properties to allow for this attrition rate. If your listing ratio is 1 in 3 (that is one listing from every three market appraisals) then you will have done 126 Market Appraisals for the year to end up with an income of $100,000. That is an average of 10/11 Market Appraisals per month.

Therefore your business begins and ends with Market Appraisals and the rest just follows! What has this got to do with Auctions, you are probably asking? Well, if you are conducting on site or in room auctions you are basically taking your business out into the street where you will meet more people, particularly the neighbours, and you will be able to show off your talents. This on its own will bring you more market appraisals which will hopefully turn into listings and then sales.

When you take on an Auction listing you will be more inclined to hand out invitations to neighbours to come to the open houses, and tell me, how many times when one For Sale sign goes up in a street do you then see two or three new signboards going up in neighbouring properties? One signboard usually creates a domino effect! But if you don't approach those neighbours they will be more inclined to call out other agents! Why? Because some people actually feel bad about 'copying' their neighbours and will avoid you altogether!! If you can get to them first, you will ease them out of this. And when they witness the great job you've done up the road, they will want to list with you. Otherwise they won't see you in action at all, and let's face it in the public's eye an agent is an agent is an agent! We know that's not so, but they don't!

Another important point is that most Real Estate office owners will be more than happy to allow you to promote yourself on a signboard or an ad if you are bringing in good marketing dollars to the office, so you have a better chance of being promoted as an individual rather than just an office. Check with your Principal, but in my experience both as a Principal and as a Consultant, I would be more than happy to allow individual promotion of an agent that's bringing in those marketing dollars! If you're the one out there doing the hard yards I'd be more than happy to let you do some self-promotion. People like dealing with people! So if the locals keep seeing your name and your face around on a few properties they will feel confident you will know what you're doing with their hard earned asset and they will want to do business with you.

In summary, never mind what kind of agent you are right now! Focus on what kind of agent you would like to become, which means you need to learn everything you can about your industry and about the different methods there are to get the job done.

Tips from this chapter:

1. **What kind of agent are you: A Handyman, A Carpenter or A Cabinet Maker?**
2. **What kind of income would you like to earn?**
3. **Work out from what you earned last year exactly how many Market Appraisals you did**
4. **If you want to give yourself a 20% pay rise this year, what do you need to do?**
5. **Keep your own statistics, become fully familiar with them – and make them work for you!**

Chapter 2:
Why Auction?

There are basically three methods that can be used to sell property. They are Private Treaty, For Sale by Tender or For Sale by Public Auction. However, there is probably a fourth method which is "Expressions of Interest" although this really falls into the Private Treaty method once a price has been agreed upon between buyer and seller. Most importantly remember this: it is your **DUTY** to work in the best interests of your clients **AT ALL TIMES!** If you are not experienced in every method of selling, then how can you say you are doing this? "Horses for courses" is a useful adage here, and emphasises the need for you to know what choice you are able to give your clients to get the best possible result for them.

Private Treaty Sale
The most common method for sale the whole World over is a sale by Private Treaty. This is when the owner, or vendor, puts an "asking price" on a property which is usually set at a figure above what the owner would like to achieve, usually with direction from we Agents, taking into account recent local comparable sale prices, which allows room for negotiation. Ideally the property is then marketed at the price we recommend (we wish!) and buyers that

Why Auction?

Chapter 2:

11

want the property will then negotiate down from this figure. Very rarely will an owner be offered more than that asking price or even at the asking price. The "game" is usually for the buyer to push that price down as hard as he can.

With this method of selling it is usual that the best offers are the first offers. The property is fresh to the market and will attract enquiry from buyers that may have been looking for some time and are ready to buy immediately. Because it is highly unlikely that any buyer will offer the full asking price, there is usually some negotiating down from that advertised figure, so it can be very difficult for an owner to accept an offer if it comes in quickly, even if that offer is at a figure that the owner first thought he would be willing to take. There will always be that nagging doubt "Did I sell too quickly?" "Did I let it go too cheaply?" "Is there a better price out there?" "What am I rushing for?" So many times I see this reaction from owners, and so many times I see these owners then selling for less than that original first offer! It can be an expensive education.

Regardless of market conditions every buyer believes that they are the only buyer on the property and they seem to make it their mission to get as much as possible off that asking price. They also want their terms and conditions met, such as, for example, a delayed settlement or a reduced settlement time. They may also insist that certain inclusions are added that were not in the contract, and their legal advisors will usually want a variety of changes to the terms specified in the owners' contract. These negotiations are usually done between the two parties through we Agents, who will be going backwards and forwards until a figure and terms are agreed upon. More often than not, the owners will have to capitulate on either their price or some of their terms if they want the sale to proceed.

Here in NSW most agents will not take a property "off the market" until a purchaser has signed a contract at the agreed price, or at their best offer. There are no "holding deposits" taken. The initial deposit has to amount to at least .25% of the purchase price, or the price offered. The agent will then take this signed contract to the owner and if the owner signs the counterpart contract, both contracts are dated and sent off to respective solicitors. This exchange is done with a cooling-off period which cannot legally be under five business days, but the cooling off time can be negotiated out further.

From the point of the contracts exchanging until the end of the cooling off period the owner is locked into that contract. He cannot change his mind about selling. He has to wait it out until the end of the cooling off period to see if his buyer can perform or even still wants to perform. This puts the owner in a very vulnerable position, particularly if he wants to purchase a property himself and needs the funds from this sale to complete his own purchase. If the purchaser changes his mind for any reason whatsoever, he does have to forfeit his original deposit (the .25%) to the owner, but often these monies are less than what the owner has to forego himself if he is upgrading to a higher price range.

Through the Private Treaty method there is no definite sale until the balance of the deposit monies are paid by 5 pm on the last business day of the cool off. This leaves the owner in limbo until this takes place and can cause a lot of stress to most vendors (and agents), particularly if they have committed themselves to another purchase. Should the sale fall through then the owner has to put the property back on the market and go through the whole agonising process again. In some unlucky instances, this may happen several times before a sale is actually finalised. By this time most owners' nerves are totally frazzled. And if this does happen what can also occur is that other savvy buyers will see the property back on the market and get even harder with their negotiations. The owner may then have no choice but to take a lesser figure than the previous sale price just to get the job done.

It has also been my experience that immediately prior to the balance of the deposit needing to be placed, some buyers will attempt to renegotiate the price once more. They may have found something in the building report that they can use as an excuse or really they will use any excuse to push the price down. I recently found out that a purchaser pushed a vendor's price down because a water tank that was never on the property when the buyer inspected the house had been removed. They firstly insisted on a $10,000 reduction – a truly ridiculous amount – which terrified the owner (who was committed to another purchase) so much so that they eagerly agreed to a $2,000 reduction. Unfortunately I didn't find out all this had happened between the solicitors until after the event otherwise I wouldn't have let this happen.

No matter how difficult this form of selling is it is still far better than before this legislation came into effect in NSW. In some instances owners literally had to wait months before a sale became unconditionally exchanged (i.e. the 10% deposit went down and the buyers were locked into the purchase or would be made to forfeit that deposit). Back when I first started in Real Estate in 1986 and through most of the 90's a fully refundable deposit would be placed on a property and in some instances properties could be off the market for many months before the sale was formalised. Imagine the stress of that! What I cannot believe is that there are many New South Wales agents out there that are **STILL** taking holding deposits and are not exchanging the contracts! Why would you do this? I know it's hard to change methodology when you are so used to it, but just think about how long matters are being drawn out if you do not have a structured time line for when things are supposed to happen! Not only is this **NOT GOOD** for your clients it is also **NOT GOOD** for your own personal income! Instead of getting paid in six weeks' time for the work you've done, this can drag out endlessly. Plus, if it does get dragged out ridiculously, you stand a chance of **LOSING THIS LISTING!** If this is you, cast your mind over the properties that were held off the market, then for some reason, the buyer pulled out and then your vendor, sick of the whole thing either pulled his property off the market or listed with another agent because your agency agreement had already expired! Even if the sale does go through eventually, how much extra time and effort did you have to put into this sale to hold the thing together? This is time wasted, better spent on prospecting for tomorrow's clients rather than worrying about yesterday's sales. Why would you do this to yourselves?

What also seems to be popular today in some areas is a Private Treaty sale but instead of a loaded price to work down, properties are being advertised with "Offers over …." Personally, I really don't like this method, I think it is highly misleading, particularly when the owner's desired price is tens of thousands of dollars higher than the figure on display. For example a good client of mine wanted to achieve $600,000 on her property. A local agent advised her that to get this she needed to advertise at "Offers over $575,000" to draw a crowd and to let them pitch against each other. As a consumer myself if I saw that price heading I would expect that an offer of $576,000 should stand a chance, not that I would have to pay at least a further $25,000 to get the property. I advertised this property at $629,000 and sold it in one day for $620,000. I doubt that the "offers over $575,000" formula would have led to a further $45,000 being offered! And even if it did, how many ticked off buyers have walked away from you, believing that you have deliberately mislead them?

For Sale by Tender

The For Sale by Tender method is very similar to the Auction system except that buyers' bids are not disclosed to each other. Sometimes this is known as a 'Silent Auction". A date will be set for all offers to be submitted and then the vendor will accept what he considers to be his best offer and terms. The successful bidder is then notified. No-one has the opportunity to make more than one bid otherwise the agent can be accused of instigating gazumping, which is illegal and can cost an agent thousands of dollars in fines and they can also lose their Licence.

What has recently become very popular, particularly in the Western Suburbs of Sydney, is a For Sale by Tender, but called a Property Launch or a Home Drive. What happens in this instance is that a property is advertised with a price range and a set open house time. No buyers will be allowed to inspect the property prior to this time frame because, again, the agent wants each buyer to see a lot of activity at the property. This will hopefully convince the buyer that there is strong competition for the property which can result in offers at the higher end of the price range or even over the price range if they are very keen.

Usually there is no more than a $30,000 play in the price range advertised such as $430,000 to $460,000, with the desired sale price approximately half way between these two figures. I have tried this method of selling and I can say it does work. However, having parameters on the price range again limits the thinking of the buyers, and in a rapidly rising marketplace, which is what we are enjoying in Sydney right now, this may prevent buyers from really stretching to get the property. And often there will be exactly the same figure offered several times, which makes me believe that if each buyer were aware of every offer, surely one of them would have paid more to get the property? Under these circumstances the owner then has to make a decision between buyers, particularly if the terms of sale are also identical.

Usually when offers are submitted through this system they are done so still with a cooling off contract and the sale is still not unconditional at the point of the owner accepting the offer. Once again the owner is in a vulnerable position.

For Sale by Public Auction

From my extensive experience I can wholeheartedly say that this sale process is the most efficient, fairest and by far the most transparent mode of selling that I have encountered.

First of all, the standard time frame for an Auction campaign is usually four weeks. During that time as many people as possible are shown the property. This can be through the weekly open houses or by appointment through the weeks leading up to Auction day. Setting the date deadlines the sale and gives both buyer and seller time to prepare for the event. This takes away any anxiety that the property has sold too cheaply or too quickly. Owners can see the volume of inspections being done and can feel safe that the very best price is going to be available on the day of the Auction.

Most importantly, when the hammer comes down at the Auction the property is **SOLD!** There is no cooling off contract, it is a definite sale at a definite price. Obviously this is very powerful for the owner. Buyers are at liberty to bid to whatever price they deem the property to be worth, but the competition is no longer against the owner and to drive his price down. The competition is to beat the other bidders and secure the property.

The terms and conditions of purchasing the property are in the Contract for Sale that the owners' solicitor has prepared and they have to be adhered to by the buyer. The buyer has the opportunity to take this contract to his own legal advisors prior to the Auction and occasionally the buyers' legal advisor will contact the sellers' solicitor to have some terms amended – but never as much as a Private Treaty sale, I've noticed.

All in all, this system puts the owner back in the driving seat, rather than the other way round. What I particularly like is that most lending bodies will take an Auction sale price as a current valuation. We are in an upwardly moving marketplace and often Property Valuers are instructed by lending bodies to look at recent **SETTLED** sales, not exchanged sales, for their benchmarks when valuing a property. These sales may have happened quite a while ago and can be considerably under immediate recent sales results. Consequently we are seeing buyers lose out on what they want if the Property Valuer comes in at a low assessment. I have recently had a purchaser agree to a purchase price of $740,000 for one of my properties. A valuer went through this property and came up with a valuation of $670,000! Fortunately the buyer did not accept this valuation and instructed his broker to change banks. The new valuer came in at $740,000, no problem, and the sale went through. I don't know how there can be a variance of $70,000 between valuers, and certainly the $670,000 figure didn't make any sense at all, but an Auction result would never have led to this outcome.

All of the above points show explicitly why this method is superior to a Private Treaty sale. I think that the reason Auctions have the edge over For Sale by Tender Sales is simply because each bidder can see what the opposition is doing, instead of trying to outguess the next person. This builds buyers confidence in the property and can encourage a stronger result for the owner. But most important of all! When that gavel comes down, the deal is done! No more running around trying to "save a sale", no sleepless nights wondering if the buyer will proceed, no properties coming back on the market. You have well and truly made a sale and can now go safely on to the next properties.

Also, there are no restrictions with an Auction sale. Let's face it, there is no scientific formula for pricing a house. Each property is totally unique and even though there may be strong comparables between houses, there can also be undetermined reasons one house is more popular than another. And that popularity can only mean one thing ... a better price for your client!

Tips from this chapter:

1. There are three basic methods of selling – do you know them all?
2. *ALWAYS* work in the best interests of the client, your ignorance is no excuse!
3. A for sale by Auction has a better chance of bringing out the very best result for your client – buyers are pitching against each other not the owner for a change.
4. Your sale won't be crashed through a poor valuation!
5. A sale by Auction puts your owner in the driving seat and leaves him there throughout the journey!

Chapter 3:

Which Clients should go to Auction?

The most important question you need to ask at a market appraisal is "Why are you selling?" The answer will be along these lines: looking to upgrade, downgrade, cash in an asset, get out of debt, end a partnership, relocate or retire to a different area. Has the recent media storm regarding the rise in home values stirred up moving needs in your client? Have they done this before, or are they fresh to the shenanigans of selling their home? Personally I have sold and bought 12 different homes to live in in my lifetime, which is the exception not the norm. However I believe that my own personal experiences of the whole traumatic process has made me a far better real estate agent. I KNOW what it's like to be on the receiving end of what I do as a job!

Your clients' motivation for why they are selling is absolutely crucial, so work out from the headings below which category they fall into.

"I'm not that motivated, but if I get my price I'll sell"

If they're not that motivated, then they probably don't think Auction is right for them. They just want to put the property on the market with a price that will test the waters. Normally half-hearted sellers will want well over market value and will only sell if they get an unusually high price. However, they may be pleasantly surprised in a rapidly rising market: they may just get their Dream Price!

I believe that even if they are not that motivated you should be willing to advise them to go through the Auction process, invest some of their own money in the promotion of their property, to test those waters. It's their choice entirely, but certainly if they really want to get their dream price and won't sell for less, then an Auction will draw out the maximum worth of their property. They don't have to sell if they're not happy with the result, but it will shorten their time on the market to find out what the market thinks of the property's value.

Do they really want to spend the next several months having people traipse through their property to then tell them "it's too dear!" or do they want to condense this into a month and find out the result quickly?

"I want to upgrade/relocate area but I haven't found what I want to buy yet"

If this is your client then they're probably scared that you may get a buyer on their home and they will have nowhere to go to. Understandable. But, what if they keep seeing homes that suit them but they're not in a position to buy and no-one will wait for them? How committed are they to making this move?

If they are absolutely sure they are moving but they cannot commit to anything until you have sold their home for them, then advise them to put the property up for Auction with a longer settlement period! Instead of the standard 6 weeks from exchanged contract to settlement, make it 12 weeks, or longer. This will give them time to sell their property and then it will give them time to look, find and secure the home they want. And whilst their own Auction programme is running, you can take them out and look at properties. They will be getting regular feedback on what buyers' are thinking their home is worth and will have better knowledge of what they can afford to spend.

Should they be relocating to a completely fresh area such as Interstate, the Coast etc. then I would strongly advise them to rent before they buy anyway. The last thing they want to do is rush to buy in an area they are completely unfamiliar with and end up with a nice home surrounded by Housing Commission properties! They would be far better off to rent for six months and get a feel for the area before committing to a purchase. They also need to get a general idea of prices in this new area. When moving away from a large city, such as Sydney, to a country/coastal/new State you will generally find prices of properties are much lower, and what may appear to be a bargain compared to their home values could actually be an over inflated price locally. Don't let them get burned.

Does this feel too risky to them? No problem. Advise them to go to their bank and discuss **Relocation Loans** with them. If they have a substantial amount of equity in their own home, generally have a good income, the chances are that they will be able to borrow the full purchase price plus all costs (such as Stamp Duty and solicitors fees). This will allow them to go out and buy before they sell and take away that feeling of vulnerability. Usually there is a time frame with this type of loan which will allow them to then sell their property, and the interest rates for this loan are usually at the same variable rate as a standard Home Loan. Once their property sells then the equity in their existing home will come off the whole amount which will either clear their debt completely or reduce it to a much lower figure. Then they need to Auction their own home to safely secure a sale within the right time frame. There is usually a set-up fee for this loan, but all this they need to discuss with their bank/lending body.

"I've already bought/built and I need to sell!"

If they are a fully committed vendor with high motivation then Auction is the only method to consider. Why? Well first of all if they are committed to another purchase and need the funds from this house to pay for the next one they need a definite time frame to work in. The Auction campaign will do that – four weeks for the programme and then their own specified time for settlement. Remember, the vendors are in control of those terms in their contract, so instead of a standard 6 weeks to settlement from exchange, they can reduce this to 5 or even 4 weeks thus reducing the waiting time for those funds to come to them, or extend this time if needs be. And when you set the Auction date you are really setting their sold date for them!

If an owner has to sell quickly then Auction will allow them to do that without necessarily compromising their price. A quick sale can often result in taking less just to make things happen. An Auction will draw out the best price regardless.

I look at price ranges for properties as being three-tiered: "Ouch!" price, if this is all you can get this hurts your plans, "Reality" price, probably what your property is really worth, "Dream" price, if you get this for your home you are ecstatic! A quick sale, or fire sale, will usually result in either an Ouch or Reality sale price. The owners are under the pump to sell and they are not in a position to negotiate hard. This is OK for an agent, but if you sincerely care about your clients, you do not want this for them.

What can be even worse is if they do go through the Private Treaty process, find a buyer and then that sale falls through, they are even more under the pump than ever before and their property's price may be compromised further. Or they could be so trapped into the sale that should the buyer put pressure on them immediately prior to the end of the cool-off they may be forced to drop their price again or stand to lose the buyer. Not a strong position to be in for them and a heck of a lot of stress for the agent looking after them.

Just remember the Golden Rule of Auction: **"Caveat Emptor!" Buyer Beware!** Simply put it is up to the purchaser to make their own enquiries and have inspections (pest and building reports etc.) done on the property prior to purchasing at Auction. If this is not done, or even if this is done and the buyer isn't happy with these reports but still goes ahead and purchases, he cannot then demand that the owner be responsible for any repairs that may need to be done to the property. The hammer comes down, that price is paid and the property is SOLD! No ifs, buts or maybes after the event. Done deal, thank you very much.

"We're divorcing/selling a Deceased Estate"

Whether it's the death of a loved one or the death of a marriage, this means that there are generally several parties involved and there can be conflict between them.

With a divorce obviously there could be acrimony between two parties which can affect sensible commercial decisions. Auctioning a property can overcome these difficulties provided that a smart reserve price is put on the property.

In the case of a Deceased Estate not only can there be conflict between beneficiaries that may increase when offers are submitted, but there is also a need to honour the memory of the person that has passed away. With an Auction you will know that you have done your very best to obtain the most out of the market to show respect to the parents or family members that have worked hard to leave them this legacy.

"I'm cashing in an investment while the prices are good"

OK. First question: have they checked with their Accountant/Financial Advisor regarding the amount of Capital Gains Tax they'll be up for? Here in Australia if a property was purchased post 1985 and that property is sold at a greater price than what was paid for it, this tax will have to be paid. I am not going to go into that arena here, I am not trained to give financial advice, and neither should you. But you can point your client in the right direction to find out if this applies to them and the consequences that may occur should they sell. It could be that they have to plan this a little better and wait for a certain time of the year. Get them to get the correct advice from an expert in that field.

Once they have researched their situation then you should recommend auctioning this asset. If the property is vacant then they really don't want it off the market for too long – chances are each month will incur expenses such as mortgage repayments, rates, maintenance etc. Or it could be vulnerable to vandalism by being vacant. So dead lining their sale will maximise their return.

Should the property be occupied by a tenant then an auction campaign should synchronise better with that occupant allowing inspections. Just a short time on a Saturday is far preferable than random inspections. And again, the best possible price will be obtained.

"I've got to sell – I can't afford to stay here!"

In this instance the quicker the property sells the better. Every month they stay on the market they are keeping an asset they cannot afford. Each month is another mortgage repayment and they get further in debt. If they've stopped paying their mortgage they are drawing closer and closer to the bank stepping in and taking the property off them.

Should they be in this position then get the property on the market immediately. Most certainly an auction is the way to go. They need to let their lending body know what action steps have been taken. The Mortgagor will also prefer an auction because this deadlines the sale and they will have a definite time frame to work with.   A **good** agent will contact that lending body and will keep them informed throughout the selling process. This will keep the wolf from the door. Don't let your client stick their head in the sand – they need to grasp the nettle!

A few years ago I was approached to sell a parcel of land that had a slab poured for a duplex. The owner of the land had entered into an agreement with her sister that she would supply the block of land and the sister and her family would build a duplex. They would then share the profits equally once the two properties were built and sold. A great plan, and should have worked perfectly.

Unfortunately the owner of the block of land had a compulsive gambling habit and the stage payments that had been made to her by the bank to fund the building project were sunk into poker machines at the local RSL rather than into the construction of the duplex. The concreter that had laid the slab hadn't been paid, the initial mortgage on the land hadn't been paid, the rates hadn't been paid and there were no further funds to finish building the dwellings. A fine mess.

I knew the circumstances were dire so I listed the property to Auction and then spent the following four weeks promoting and showing the property as is my job. I arranged for the two sisters to come into my office the day before the auction to set the reserve price. The owner of the block came in with handfuls of unopened mail from the bank she was with. She was in such a deep hole she didn't even have the wherewithal to open her mail, so I did it for her. It was at that point that we all discovered that the bank had already moved on her and repossessed the property!

Long story short, I got onto the bank and got a stay of execution. I took the property to auction the next day and got the absolute most out of the buyer. We did not exchange under auction conditions (we raised the reserve price to a figure that cleared all debt which was a considerable amount over market value). I obtained a signed contract off that buyer with the 10% deposit, explaining to him that he needed to wait for an answer and if it was a "yes" then the exchange would be under cooling off terms. I then got hold of her Super fund, applied for a release of some funds because of her extenuating circumstances, filled out forms and got the evidence of the debt she was in and managed to get sufficient funds released to clear all her remaining debts. If the bank had gone through with the repossession they would have auctioned the property as a fire sale and most likely would have sold the property at a much lower figure than I achieved. There would have been further interest charges from the take-over to the sale end and all the costs associated with the sale would have been passed on to the owner. So even though the property would have been taken off the owner, once the property is sold the owner is still responsible for the shortfall between the sale price and all debts to the lending body. She would end up with an extremely bad credit rating and still have been in debt to the concreter, local Council et al.

So, don't let your client stick their head in the sand. If holding onto the property is ruining the quality of their life and sinking them further into debt, get them to grasp the nettle, get it sold, and get back onto solid ground. And do it quickly whilst they still have some leverage. Tell them to avoid a repossession at all costs, the consequences could stay with them for a very long time.

Tips from this chapter:

1. No matter what their motivation an Auction is a suitable way to sell
2. The owner retains the control of the sale throughout the Auction process
3. The terms and conditions of the Contract can be set to suit their needs
4. Get your client to do his homework – get legal advice or financial advice first and foremost
5. Do they want to deadline the sale of their home without sacrificing their price? Then take their property to Auction!

Chapter 4:
Marketing the Property

So, you have convinced the client to list their property with you for Auction. Well done! But before you even go to the market appraisal you will need to have prepared Marketing Programmes for the Auction Campaigns.

Usually these campaigns are three tiered and called something like "Bronze", "Silver" or "Gold" or something similar. And the campaign fees will increase with each package, depending on the extras included. Marketing packages will vary between different suburbs and States depending on the use or not of print advertising.

The standard campaigns comprise of professional photography, Virtual Tours and floor plans; advertising on the major internet sites; sometimes print advertising in local papers; personalised signboards with photographic displays of internal features of the property; professionally produced leaflets of the property and, of course, the Auctioneer's fee.

With the advent of Internet advertising a lot of print advertising has been made obsolete in many suburbs close into City centres. It was always extremely expensive in these areas and now is certainly not essential for a good marketing campaign.

There are several major internet sites that serve us here in Australia such as realestate.com and domain.com. I like a presence in both as they are both high traffic portals to properties.
Both sites, for extra fees, will allow a property to be featured as a header on the front page of the site for a particular suburb. Sometimes these fees will be part of the auction campaign packages being offered, but you can do them as add-ons.

I truly believe that if you are going to take a property to Auction you need to broadcast this as wide and as far as you can. You want to capture every single person looking to buy in this price range, and you want them to come through this property. If owners are prepared to spend money on preparing their home for market – and I meet a lot of home owners ready to paint and recarpet their homes to make them look more attractive to buyers – then doesn't it make sense that they would spend money to promote their property? As Agents we will have standard amounts we can invest in the promotions, but no agent is going to invest thousands of his dollars into a home's promotion – that is for the owner to do. It doesn't have to be thousands but it will be money well spent!

Whichever auction campaign is chosen, it should have a four week lifespan. I have tried three week campaigns – not bad, but really not enough time to heavily promote, and five week auctions are just too long. Most buyers won't wait this long and will look for something else.

Standard practice is to hold an open house each Saturday at the same allotted time. With on-site auctions (auctions that are actually held at the property) the actual auction usually takes place immediately after the last open house. With in-rooms auctions (groups of properties are put together and auctioned in possibly a community hall, at a local club or in the agency's office) the auction is usually held on an evening (Thursday evening seems to be popular) after the last Saturday open house.

With in-room auctions an "order of sale" needs to be available on the night showing the order that the auctioneer is going to call the auctions. Standard practice, if there are several properties up for auction on the same night, is to have the most popular at the beginning and at the end so that good results are obtained at the beginning to set the mood for the evening and then also to keep the crowd in the room. When I used to call auctions for other agents I have called as many as 20 auctions in one night! As you can imagine, I didn't spend too much time on each individual property – there just wasn't the time to do this. We would start at 7 pm and we had to be finished by 11 pm – that's when the room closed. So that meant calling 5 auctions per hour. Doable, certainly, but very little individual attention to each property. In-rooms auctions will have videos of each individual property playing immediately prior to the auctioneer starting to call that particular auction.

Personally I prefer on-site auctions. The reason I do so is because I allow at least an hour for each property. I can spend time talking with owners so that we can plan our strategy (more about that later), then I can call the auction. I am not under pressure to move on to the next property, so I can really make sure I extract the juice for my owner before I bring the gavel down.

With in-rooms auctions, my attention is to get through the volume of properties. However, I have to say that occasionally with in-room auctions buyers may start bidding on properties they haven't physically seen! I have had several "sight unseen" sales at these venues. Usually a buyer that has missed out on an earlier auction will stay in the rooms, sees something else he quite likes and then starts to bid. He has come to the venue to buy and that's exactly what he does! It can be dangerous, because he hasn't done his research, may not know the location or if there are any detrimental aspects to the property, and is taking quite a risk. There is nothing detrimental to the owner; "Caveat Emptor!" Buyer Beware!" He has sold, and that's all he wants to do. As far as you the agent is concerned, it is an unbelievable result! With all the running around we have to do for buyers in any other method of sale, this is as easy as could be!

I can unequivocally say that selling "sight unseen" only ever happens with an Auction. With any other form of selling it is unheard of. It usually takes several inspections with a Private Treaty sale for the buyer to make an offer and even then they have a cooling-off period in which they can change their mind.

Going back to the marketing of the property please remember this: the initial impression a buyer is going to have of the property is through the promotional or marketing material. It needs to be sharp, well written, well photographed and prominently displayed. It needs to capture the main selling features of the property and it needs to create urgency or the willingness to act within the buyer.

The heading of the ad really needs to capture, in just a handful of words, enough interest to make a buyer find out more about the property and the reason it's for sale. Some agents will use an opening bid or starting bid on a flash on the photo. This can be most useful to draw a crowd. Usually the opening/starting bid is approximately 10%-20% under the anticipated sale price, but it can direct the right interest to the property and is a good benchmark to give buyers so that they can check if the property is within their budget.

The owner's reason for selling is also important as it will show the buyer how motivated they are. All buyers want to make sure that owners will be realistic in their expectations on the day of the auction, otherwise there is no point in attending the auction. They may be willing to pay a big price through the competitive bidding, but they want to know that they do stand a chance of buying the property, so they do like to be given guidelines. The best auction results are usually obtained when the owner's expectations are similar to the crowds. That's when the competitive bidding really does kick in.

Probably one of the best auctions that I remember was one in the late 1980's of a property that was in a flood affected area local to my office. The owner was moving to Townsville and wanted a quick sale. I assessed the property to be worth approximately $100,000 to $110,000 at that time. The owner told me he was very happy to take $95,000 as this sum would enable him to do what he wanted.

I've never been the sort of agent that would simply go and get that figure, knowing it was selling the property under market value. I have always tried to get the very best price for my clients. I strongly urged him to go to auction and I asked his permission to use the heading "Reserve Price set at $95,000!" which he allowed me to do. I literally had dozens of buyers' clambouring for the property during the campaign, with most of them wanting to buy immediately. I advised my client to wait until Auction and not to consider selling beforehand, which he did.

On the night of the auction there were dozens of people wanting this property. Immediately prior to the auction the owner came up to me and said:

"Oh Maria! I had a beautiful dream last night! I dreamt that my house sold for $115,000!"

Well it did sell, but not for $115,000. It sold for $137,500! My owner was ecstatic! Now THAT'S what I get paid for. Not just selling the house, but really working out what is the most favourable strategy to get the very best result for my client. Oh, and by the way, this listing is the sort I can spruik about, and of course it brought in more listings!

Only last week I was paid the biggest compliment of my career. I received an email from a lady living in USA. The email read:

"Hi Maria,
I've been trying to find you. You sold my property at …………….. back in 2009. I need to sell my mother's

house and I told my brothers if there is one person that will get us the best price it's Maria!"

This lady had searched through Google to find me. Wow! And I most certainly did remember her and I vividly remembered the auction I promoted and called for her. She was living in the USA back then also and family members were living rent free in her house. And they had trashed it. This was when I was working out of one of my own offices under a different banner, before I had decided to semi-retire (!). I assessed the value to be approximately $300,000 to $320,000 at that time taking into consideration the amount of work needed to bring this property back to a well presented state and I suggested auction to her, which she agreed to do. I marketed the property with the heading along the lines of "Renovate or Detonate!" and had an opening bid on the property of $270,000.

Immediately prior to the auction I received an offer on the property of $340,000 – an excellent price. By now this lady had returned to Australia for the actual auction. I can remember sitting on her mother's back porch showing her the signed contract at $340,000 and the 10% deposit cheque that I had brought with me. She asked me for advice, but I refused to give it to her – I told her that I didn't want to be responsible for the decision, it was her call. Cleverly, she reworded the question:

"Ok, so what would you do if you were me?" she asked

"Personally, I would wait for the auction." Was my reply. "But I'm not advising you to do that. And if you do decide to go to auction, we should still keep your reserve price at $320,000 as we've already discussed. So you may not get $340,000 on the day of the auction. And if I tell you not to take this offer and wait for the auction and your home only sells for $320,000, I could have just cost you $20,000!" I explained.

"I hear you. But you know what? I like what you said about waiting for the auction. If I lose money, well that's my fault, not yours." She kindly replied.

So the following Saturday we held the auction. And we sold her home for $375,000! And all these years later she wants me to work for her so much that she was willing to search for me!

Tips from this chapter:

1. Have at least three campaigns ready to offer your clients, and have add on benefits that they can choose if they so wish
2. Make sure the advertising really captures either the essence of the property or their determination to sell
3. If the clients are prepared to spend money getting the home looking "right" to the buyers, then also make sure that they don't skimp on its promotion
4. Work out a strategy with your clients – and make sure they approve your ads
5. Remember, a well-strategized campaign can bring tens of thousands of dollars return!

Chapter 5:
Conducting the Open House

Organise a Contract for Sale

First and foremost your client needs to have a contract for sale before the property can be advertised, so you need to advise them to contact a solicitor as soon as possible. Depending on the speed of your local Council, this document can be prepared in as little as two days or up to two weeks. Without this document you cannot promote the property, so get them to order this straight away.

Whilst this document is being prepared you can get professional photography, Virtual Tours, floor plans and personalised signboards organised. Once the contract comes in you can get the property on the market straight away.

Tell your owners to get the home looking good!

The best advice you can give your owners is to suggest this: "if you were about to sell your car you would probably get it detailed before you advertise it. Think the same way about your property." Most homes today are beautifully presented, but I still come across those that aren't, and this can cost the owner thousands of dollars. There is nothing more off-putting to a buyer than the thought of cleaning up somebody else's mess. And I believe it is our duty as a conscientious agent to let our owners know this, subtly.

Over the years I have seen some really filthy houses! And yet these owners expect to get the same result as pristine clean homes. I have been through houses that have had dirty underwear strewn over bedroom floors (on the day of the auction too, I might add) and have had to kick stuff I'd rather not touch under beds!! I often shake my head with disbelief when this happens. I understand that we are all very busy people, and I understand that children and pets leave their debris behind them, but put yourself in the minds of the buyers. If an owner doesn't have time to do this themselves, get them to get a cleaner in! Most agents that have rent rolls will also have cleaners on their books that will give a home a good clean for just a few hundred dollars – money well spent, I can assure you. Advise your clients to get windows and carpets cleaned, de-clutter the home, get the gardens trimmed, lawns cut, edges done, and weeding done. And please get this done BEFORE the photography is due so that the property is looking good before it ever comes on the market. If they leave it and only get it done for the day of the auction they have already missed the boat! And if there is anything else you believe will help your clients sell their home, tell them!

Dogs and cats in the house? Not a good idea when we are selling their home. Advise them to keep their pets and their "stuff" (i.e. beds and bowls) outside for at least the duration of the open house or reinspection. I love dogs, but they are smelly creatures even when they are bathed regularly. There are many people out there totally averse to keeping pets in the house and they can get very turned off your property. And we have a lot of people out there today with allergies that are sparked by pets – don't let them get turned off!

Open for Inspection

It's Saturday, open house day. No doubt your clients have been thoroughly scrubbing up all week just for this half hour window of opportunity. I have heard owners advised to "brew coffee" "bake a cake" or "light scented candles" – I don't subscribe to these points of view. There are people that are allergic to certain scents or that are nauseated by the smell of coffee or baking. My suggestion is that a home should smell **CLEAN!** Cleaning agents, floor cleaners, disinfectants are far preferable aromas than anything else. If your clients are smokers or there have been pets in the home they really need to let the fresh air in and either get rid of or get cleaned any of the fabrics that can harbour these smells. Curtains are often culprits in holding in stale smells – get your clients to get them washed or dry cleaned well in advance. Perfumes and baking smells will only mask a bad aroma, not get rid of it.

A tip for actors before they go onto stage is "check your nose and flies"! With a home I always suggest "check your toilets" before an open house, particularly if little ones live there! So it is advisable for you the agent to arrive about five minutes before the open house starts so you can do a quick walk through and check what's necessary. By the way, if you are decidedly late for an open house, did you know that the client can expect to be reimbursed his marketing fees? Try to explain that to your principal!! There really is no excuse for being late for anything. If you are trying to cram too much in at the same time, you will not give a quality level of service and you will lose clients.

In my opinion it is entirely up to the owner whether or not they want to be present whilst the open house is taking place. Many owners don't want to be there and will disappear for the duration, but if they ask me if I want them to leave then I tell them it's up to them. All I do advise is that they don't follow the buyers around trying to be helpful and that they don't engage buyers in long conversations about how great their property is. This often smacks of desperation, and this is not what we want the buyers to believe. If your client decides not to be there then reassure him that we agents will look after their property like it is ours. We don't allow people to just open cupboard doors, drawers or closets. If they want a closer look at the size of any storage areas we suggest that they do a reinspection to do this.

I rarely hold an open home singlehandedly. Usually there at least two of us, one at the front door to take down buyers' details and one inside to answer questions and observe the behaviour of the buyers. Nevertheless, please advise your clients not to leave jewellery, money or small objects of value lying around, it can be too tempting. I have never had anything stolen at an open house in all these years, most people are extremely honest, but I never chance fate.

Personally I will not allow a buyer to enter an occupied home unless they have given me their name and contact details. Very occasionally I do come across people that strongly object to doing this (goodness knows why!) and they simply are not allowed to enter the premises. I also make sure I get buyers to take their shoes off on wet days or to walk on carpeted areas. Leaving old towels at the front and back doors on rainy days would be really useful if you can remind your client to do this. I also will not allow too many people through the property at the same time. There has to be a limit to how many people are in the property simply because a large crowd will make any property seem small and can be

Chapter 5:   Conducting the Open House

off-putting. How can you really see the home if you can't see beyond other peoples' bodies?!!

Generally speaking you need to try to get buyers' opinions when they walk back out of the house and this feedback is extremely important for you to pass on to the owner. If there have been droves of people through the home then we may have to wait until later that day or Monday to get that feedback. My standard practice is to both telephone the owner later that day/Monday to give them the numbers of inspections and to let them know how many people are interested in attending the auction. I will also send a written report to the owners during the course of the following week with the buyer's name, his opinion of value and his general comments about the property. This information is invaluable, particularly when it comes to setting the reserve price. Remember, these buyers will be seeing everything in this price range and will be comparing properties. We agents see our stock, not the stock being promoted by our competition, so our vision is limited.

Assessing the Interest in the Home
As an agent I generally look at the number of contracts that have been issued for the property as a guideline to the volume of people that may be interested in coming to the auction. Usually when we are asking buyers what they think of the property we should also ask them if they will be coming to the auction to bid. Generally we can pick the keen buyers

and the half-hearted buyers at this stage, and we need to convey this feedback to the owner.

Sometimes we will get offers prior to the auction and I shall discuss this in greater depth in the next chapter. Obviously if people are making offers then they are keen and one would assume that they would be coming to the auction if their offer is declined.

Another good way to assess interest is from the pest and or building reports that are requested prior to the auction, although far more rare than it really should be. I have had many, many successful auctions where no reports are done whatsoever. I actually do advise buyers to get at least a pest report done, but they often don't listen to this advice! Of the 21 properties I sold under the hammer last year *less than half* had pest reports done on them before the auction! And very, very, very occasionally a buyer might get a valuation done on the property.

Regardless of all this, you can get buyers turning up on the day of the auction that have never seen the property before that successfully bid and blow everyone else out of the water. This happens more frequently than not, and no longer surprises me as much as it used to. Like I said earlier, I have even experienced buyers buying off slides/videos that have never seen the property until they become the owners! Only with an auction ….

But please remember this: the **MOST IMPORTANT THING** you can do as an agent during the Auction campaign is to give your owners constant **FEEDBACK** both verbally and in writing.

Tips from this chapter

1. The owner needs to get a Contract for Sale prepared by their solicitor/conveyancer
2. All cleaning and repair work done needs to be done before the photography is taken.
3. Let your client know if there is anything that needs particular attention
4. Professional cleaners are available if your client doesn't have time to freshen the house himself
5. Pets and their "stuff" need to be kept outdoors during open house inspections
6. Check the toilets before the open house starts
7. If you're clients are staying home, don't let them follow the buyers around
8. Give detailed feedback from the buyers – particularly written reports
9. Check the volume of contracts issued and reports done to assess the interest in the property
10. Constantly update your owners with the thoughts and the opinions of all buyers.

Chapter 6:
Handling Offers before the Auction

The most frequently asked question buyers ask is "how much will the owners take?" and this is why I never want the reserve price set until the week of the auction, because what the owner will take as opposed to what a competitive crowd may yield can be several thousands of dollars apart. If I tell a buyer what the owner wants it will either put him off completely or it could strongly influence his opinion of the property's value.

The whole point of an auction is to see how much buyers, with competition, will pay. I usually give buyers a general guideline with some examples of what has recently sold locally or I will give a guideline by saying "we're expecting a sale over ...." I will then follow that up with "what is your price range?" If they are well under the owner's thinking, I will not encourage these buyers to come to the auction – why waste their time by getting their hopes too high?

Keen buyers will then try to buy prior to the auction and some will submit solid offers during the campaign. Their general thinking is to secure the property for themselves and to shut the door on their competition. However, the majority of buyers make offers that equate to a reality based price, not a dream price for the owner, which is what an auction is really all about.

For example, I recently had an auction where the owner told me at the point of listing that they would be more than happy with $620,000. We could have easily listed this property at say, $629,000 and had it sold within one day at $620,000. Instead of doing this I strongly urged them to take the property to auction. During the campaign I could see there were several really interested parties that really wanted to buy and it would have been easy to sell to any of them for $620,000 prior to the auction. The owner would have got what they wanted and I would have made a very quick sale. However, rather than do this I encouraged the owner to wait until the auction. We still set the reserve price at $620,000, and I brought the hammer down at $655,000 – a nice windfall for any owner. Had the owner not listened to my advice he would have sold for $620,000 and never known that he had missed out on $35,000!

When buyers ask me if an owner will sell before auction I always explain that for an owner to do this, he must be seduced by that offer, it must be in or very close to his Dream Price range. Then we go round in circles for a little bit whilst the buyer tries to pull the owner's price out of me and I try to pull his best price out of him. It's an inevitable dance which usually ends with the buyer making an offer. I generally then say "that's quite a reasonable offer but it may not seduce the owner to cancel everything and sell to you. However, he may willingly take this on the day" because I don't want to lose this buyer completely. We need as many bidders to attend the auction as possible. There will only be one buyer, the rest of the field will drive up the price.

I work for the owner, not the buyer, and my mission is to get the very best price out of the marketplace. The buyer's mission is to drive the price down or to eliminate the competition. However, I must submit all offers to the owners – that's the law – it is not for me to make decisions on behalf of the owners. I will always tell the owners what offers have been submitted not only because I am legally obliged to do so, but also this information is imperative when we sit and set the reserve price.

So when these offers are being made to you don't be disappointed. Many offers prior to an auction - even low offers – are an indication of how many people are interested in the property. The more the better. Most buyers still won't listen to the agent and will still make low offers – their mission is to push the price down. Not many buyers will submit their very best offer prior to an auction. In some instances, even **they** don't know what their very best price is until they are pushed by the competition.

I recently called an auction where a buyer came to the property on the first open house and was extremely keen to buy it and he indicated that he would pay $530,000, but wouldn't make an offer over this. The listing agent believed that the property was worth $530,000 to $550,000. The owner was happy to sell at $530,000 as he was committed to buying a business and this price allowed him to fulfil his obligations. Following the agent's advice the owner didn't accept the offer of $530,000 prior to the auction but he did set the reserve price at $530,000. On the day of the auction there were only four registered bidders, the keen buyer, two half-hearted buyers and a completely new contender that had not viewed the property before that day. The bidding started slowly and it was like pulling teeth until I announced that the property was on the market when we eventually hit $530,000. Suddenly the new contender started to bid and would not let go! His final and winning bid was $611,000, and the very keen bidder's last bid was $610,000! He had gone $80,000 OVER what he offered prior to auction! However, I do believe that had he made an offer of $580,000 prior to the auction, the owner would have been tempted to take this. I doubt when he was making his offer he never even dreamt that under pressure he would have gone to $610,000.

When a good offer comes along before an auction, it is the hardest thing as an agent to advise an owner one way or another. This must be entirely their choice. However, I really do believe that if there has been a lot of interest in the property and several contracts have been handed out there is a strong possibility that the auction will yield more. I am always far more inclined to suggest that an owner waits for the auction rather than sells beforehand, but it's not my money that I am risking. As in the example in Chapter 4, had that owner accepted the offer of $340,000, which was $20,000 over what she was hoping to get, she would have missed out on a sale price of $375,000! Her decision earned her and extra $35,000 – big money.

As you can see, I am a devotee of waiting til the day rather than making a quick sale. I can really only remember, over all these years and over all these sales, when an owner sold to the same buyer that offered prior to the auction for a lesser figure, and that lesser figure was only down by $1,000. And I have to say I have gotten more listings during a full auction campaign and an auction at the front of a house than I ever have a quick sale that was done behind closed doors. This is a WIN-WIN situation for the owner and for you.

So when you are presented with a good offer make sure you also let your client know how many buyers there are on the property. Let your clients know how many contracts have been issued. If this offer is at or very close to your clients Dream Price, then do tell them to give it serious consideration. Ask them if they will find it easy to live with the consequences should they reject this offer and then sell for less.

If they do decide to accept this offer, don't take the property off the market or cancel any of the open houses until the buyer has presented you with an unconditionally signed contract and the 10% deposit. **DO NOT** accept a contract with a cooling-off period. This would only be useful to the buyer, not to the seller. And, just to be on the safe side, **DO NOT** tell any of the other buyers that an offer has been accepted. If this buyer gets remorse and changes his mind, you don't want to have lost other buyers' interest. You will get some annoyed parties if this property does sell prior to auction, so expect a backlash. My answer is always "why didn't you make an offer? The property has been available and you have had an opportunity to buy before auction, but you didn't take any action. It was the owner's decision to sell, and that is his prerogative."

Please remember that as an agent we can be heavily fined or lose our licence if we encourage gazumping. This means we cannot go to all the other interested parties and tell them the amount that we've just been offered to try and get more. If your clients are thinking like this, then tell them to reject this offer and wait for the auction.

Here is another cautionary tale: many buyers will do almost anything to find out what the owner will take. I had a listing several years ago that I was auctioning. We were at the end of the campaign and we had a reasonable amount of interest in the property even though we were in a flat market at the time. The owner rang me the week of the auction and he was really upset. I asked him what was wrong and he said:

"One of the buyers came back last night and knocked on the door. He wanted to have another look through. I'd seen him at the open house so I thought it'd be OK without getting you out here." He said.

"That's your choice, but I would have been happy to come if you rang me. But what's upset you so much?" I replied.

"Well, I showed him around for a bit and then he said "I'm thinking of paying $180,000 for this, is that OK?" and I said "No it bloody well isn't! I won't sell for a cent under $220,000!" If that's all he's thinking why are you letting him come to the auction?" He exploded, angrily.

My owner had fallen for the oldest trick in the book. "Throw an offer at the owner and if he is naïve or if you catch him off guard, he will tell you what he wants to get for the property!" I smoothed down my owner and told him this, nicely. The outcome? This buyer came to the auction and paid $225,000 for the property.

The moral of the story is simple, tell your owner to never disclose what he wants for the property. Explain that he must tell no-one and do not be lured into giving the game away. If someone throws an offer do not over-react! Should buyers come to the property without an appointment it is the owner's choice whether or not he is willing to let them in, but if he is paying an agent a selling fee then it is more than reasonable to expect the buyer to inspect with the agent. If a buyer does turn up out of hours, sure an owner can let him inspect if he wants to, but don't get drawn into talking about the price. Some buyers will try to "win you over" hoping that if the owner likes them they will sell it them before the auction or for a cheaper amount. Don't let your client be swayed by this! This is your client's chance to maximise his return: he doesn't owe anyone any favours. And tell your owner to be careful who he confides in – neighbours and friends might know interested parties!!!

Tips from this chapter:

1. All buyers will want to know how much the owner wants and if he'll sell before auction. It is their mission to push the price down, it is the agent's mission to get the owner the best price.
2. Don't be disappointed by low offers before the auction. The competition between the buyers will bring the best price regardless of what they say before the auction.
3. If your owners are too tempted and they do take an offer prior to auction, it MUST be an unconditional offer with a 10% deposit. DO NOT TAKE YOUR PROPERTY OFF THE MARKET WHILST THIS SALE GOES THROUGH.
4. Don't ring all other interested parties to try and drive the price up. Firstly, it is illegal for an agent to encourage gazumping. Secondly if this buyer gets remorse and doesn't proceed it could ruin your owner's chance at auction.
5. Be careful that your owner is not lured to give away what the anticipated reserve price will be. Don't overreact to silly offers.
6. Don't let your owners be charmed into a sale. This is their opportunity to maximise their return and they are not obliged to do anyone any favours.

Chapter 7:
Setting the Reserve Price

Reserve Price

All agents work in different ways, but I prefer to leave setting the reserve price to the week of the auction. I think it is imperative to really study the feedback from the buyers and to intelligently work out a strategy.

At the point of listing there would have been a discussion about the price range the agent believed the property fell into and the owner would have given him their expectations. Your opinion would have been recorded on the front page of your agency agreement. I think it is most important to refer back to this. Unless there have been some severe economic changes in the marketplace since this was done, such as interest rate rises, these figures should still be relevant. If the interest rates have just dropped that may not automatically raise the value of the property. There is always a knee-jerk reaction to rates going up but not down, and it is a viable reaction. If the interest rates rise, then a buyer's buying power goes down. Fear also plays a part in the buyer's mind – "will I afford my loan if the rates keep rising?" etc.

I will never forget driving down to the Masonic Hall in Liverpool in June 1989 for our auction night. I had three listings myself that night and there were collectively a further twelve properties going to the auction block. We had several buyers on all of our properties and we were gearing up for a fantastic night. The auctions were starting at 7 pm. I was driving down to the venue to prepare the room and the 6 o'clock news came on the car radio. Interest rates had just risen to 17%! BANG! In one instant the market collapsed and we then went into "the recession we had to have". **NOT ONE** of our properties sold that night. **NOT ONE!** The buyers that did turn up didn't make a bid. Every single property was passed in with no bids. I had never seen anything like it. It totally scared me.

It took a long time to recover from this marketplace. There were many repossessed properties coming onto the market and the prices were falling away badly. Auctions were still a good way to sell, **PROVIDED THAT** the reserve prices were set sensibly.

And even in a hot market, which we are enjoying right now in Australia, the reserve prices must still be set sensibly. Just because droves of people have gone through the property don't let your owner be fooled into making his Dream Price the reserve price.

It is better to discuss the reserve price with your client in the privacy of their home or your office before the day of the auction where there are no prying ears and you can be very open with your conversation. I always speak with every person that has inspected this property prior to this meeting. I will be very direct and ask them if they intend to attend the auction and if they intend to bid. They will then give me a very direct response; yes they are coming and they will be bidding; they are coming to observe but will not be bidding or they are not coming at all. I usually have a list of names in front of me and I colour code the responses. This gives me a quick reference to the definite number of buyers that are coming and that intend to bid. More often than not the keener buyers have had their solicitors contact the owners' solicitors to alter some of the conditions in the contract or to alter the deposit amount. They may also have had pest and building inspections done on the property, but not always. In fact more often than not, no reports will be done.

The best advice I can give you at this stage is stick to the game plan. Don't move the goal posts unless your client has really changed his mind about selling. The ideal reserve price should act as a **trigger** for competitive bidding so it needs to be set at the lower end of the Reality range. In fact what you should advise your client to do is seriously consider the very, very lowest price he is prepared to accept and **SET THAT** as the reserve price.

Why? Like I said, you want this to act as a trigger, not the brakes. Many people attend auctions, register to bid and do nothing until the Auctioneer declares "this is on the market, I'm selling today". Once this declaration is made a surprising number of people then start bidding. There is no guarantee, however. If the bidding stops at that figure, your owner is **SOLD** and has to accept this is what the buying public believe the property is worth today. **An owner cannot refuse to sell once the reserve price is hit**.

The volume of inspections can be a good yardstick to see how popular this style of home is with current buyers, but volume doesn't always mean vast numbers of people registering to bid. One recent auction listing I had in Turramurra brought in 45 inspections, over 20 contracts were issued on the property (thank goodness for email otherwise we would have annihilated a small forest!) yet on the day of the auction there were only seven registered bidders. The vendor was sensible, we stuck to the game plan and kept the reserve price low, and we ended up with $95,000 over that reserve price, which was a further $45,000 more than what we both agreed we would like the property to sell for.   The winning buyer was involved in the bidding from the get-go, but two bidders didn't join in until the property was on the market, which then drew the best price out of that buyer.

If your owner is reluctant to take a risk or if he prefer to make his final decision whilst the property is being auctioned, then set a higher reserve price than this lowest figure, but explain to him to be prepared to drop down from that during the auction if the bidding stops and he is happy to take the last bid offered. Getting the property on the market is absolutely crucial to not only making a sale, but in getting the juice out of the buyers. So many times the bidding stops prior to that reserve price, the owners then put the property on the market and it fires up the bidding once more. There is no guarantee that this will happen, but here are a few examples:

1. Vendor advised that reserve price should be set at $700,000. Reserve price set at $735,000. Bidding stopped at $700,000. Vendor put property on the market **new bidder stepped in at this stage** and property sold for $706,000.
2. Vendor advised that reserve price should be set at $500,000. Reserve price set at $550,000. Bidding stopped at $521,000. Vendor put property on the market and property sold for $530,000.
3. Vendor advised that reserve price should be set at $510,000. Reserve price set at $540,000. Bidding stopped at $515,000. Vendor put property on the market, **new bidder stepped in at this stage** and property sold for $536,000.

As you can see from the above example, new bidders stepped in **once the property was on the market.** Had these owners not dropped their reserve prices and allowed the property to be passed in, chances are they would not have gotten the final price because the competition would have then reverted to being between buyer and seller, not between buyer and buyer.

I believe that the setting of the reserve price is actually indicative of how much an owner trusts his agent. If they believe in their agent, then they also believe that he is determined to get the very best price. Why? Well commercially an agent will use this result to impress other owners thinking of selling (not surprisingly many would-be sellers attend auctions to see how an agent will perform) and when the public see success they will give their business to that agent. They won't be impressed if they feel that the property undersold. More importantly, good agents have a professional pride in what they do. For them it's not just about making a sale, but it's also the self-satisfaction that no-one else could have done a better job. "Tradesmen" agents probably wouldn't even have suggested auction to a vendor, or will try to turn them off auction; "Carpenter" agents just want the hammer to come down; "Cabinet Maker" agents take a real pride to go above and beyond their clients expectations, with the way the marketing is done, the way the campaign is organised, in getting the very, very best price for their clients and then, finally to take away all obstacles between the exchange of contracts to moving out day. So what type of agent are you?

As an auctioneer my greatest thrill is to go way above reserve price for the owners. When I called auctions for other agents I would always have a discussion with each owner prior to the auction starting, whether the auctions were in rooms or on site. I wanted to make sure that their agent had covered everything with them and I also wanted to reassure them that I never bring the hammer down quickly. Never. I need to know myself that there is not another cent out there that I haven't captured. The highest amount I have ever achieved over reserve price is *$600,000!!* The final sale figure was actually almost double the reserve price and my proudest moment as an auctioneer! What is important to note here is that this particular property had had two independent Valuers submit valuations on this property and the owners based their reserve price on these expert opinions.

I will discuss later about dropping the reserve price as the auction is underway, but the time for clients to discuss this between partners in the property is from the time you have set the reserve price to the actual auction taking place. Tell your clients to really nut out the absolute minimum they are prepared to take – don't leave this undiscussed until the auction is happening! Good old scouting adage: "Be Prepared".

Better this discussion is superfluous and the bidding sails past the reserve rather than having to make tough, hard decisions in the moment.

Dropping the Reserve Price at Auction

I always run through all scenarios with my owners before the day of the auction, and the most important ground I believe I need to cover, even if I get a reserve price that I am happy with, is what can happen on the day if we don't reach that reserve price.

The bidding stops: we are say just a few thousand dollars short of that reserve; I stop the auction and seek my owner's instructions. Decision time. Can I call this property "On the market" and make the sale, or do I pass it in? This really is a most critical decision. Some owners believe that they are better off passing the property in and negotiating with the highest bidder after the auction: **ABSOLUTELY NOT!** In all the times I have had this happen I find that the buyers are less likely to improve their offer significantly after the auction. They feel that they are back in the driving seat and become more entrenched in their price. But worse than this, you are only negotiating with one buyer – the rest of the field are shut out.

A really good example of this I recorded in my first book *"Auction Success – Top 10 Tips to Successfully Buy a Property @ Auction"*. One of my vendors went to an auction to buy once I had unconditionally exchanged her sale. She stopped bidding for a particular property at $585,000 – the reserve price wasn't reached. Like all good agents, the selling agent then went between buyer and seller and told my client that if she increased her bid by $1,000 to $586,000 the owner would put the property on the market. She did as directed, the Auctioneer declared her increased bid and declared the property was "on the market." Then a person in the crowd who wasn't even registered at that point, indicated that he wanted to bid. The Auctioneer, correctly, stopped the auction, allowed the new contender to register and then accepted his bid of $590,000! My vendor couldn't afford to go higher than this bid and consequently missed out on the property.

Getting the property "on the market" during the auction is so much more effective to draw out the best price rather than trying to negotiate after the auction. In the above example had that bidder not gone the extra $1,000 before the end of the auction and the owner had been rigid in not dropping the reserve price to $585,000, the new contender would never have gotten involved and the owner would have missed out on a further $4,000.

Vendor Bid

As I have mentioned before, I really don't like using this unless I absolutely have to. I consider that the only time I need to draw on this is if the bidding has stopped too far away from the reserve price and negotiating with the under bidder and the owner hasn't reached a positive conclusion.

The only other time I want to use a Vendor Bid is if there is only one registered bidder. I have sold a considerable number of auctions under the hammer where this has happened. Usually what will happen is the one and only buyer will make an opening bid, I counter with a vendor bid, and they bid again at a figure the owner will accept. If the bidder doesn't make an opening bid, then I will make the opening bid with the Vendor Bid and then declare that the next bid will be the buying bid.

Consequently I always advise my vendors that I want to be able to call a Vendor Bid and then declare that the next bid will be the buying bid, otherwise it is extremely difficult to get another bid.

Another thing to note is that if a property is passed in and any one enquires "what did the property get passed in at?" in New South Wales we cannot declare the Vendor Bid, but we have to declare the actual bid made by the last buyer.

Tips from this chapter:

1. Remember: the Reserve Price should act like a trigger to the bidding, not the brakes!
2. Don't let your client move the goalposts unless he doesn't want to sell!
3. When setting the reserve price go back to the agency agreement and refer to the prices discussed at the start of the campaign.
4. Don't let your client get carried away because he has seen volumes of buyers go through the property – so many owners get over excited and make their Dream Price their reserve price.
5. Top professionals want a great result too! Make sure your owner knows this.
6. Always have a Plan B so that there is a fall-back position if the reserve price isn't reached and get this well and truly discussed BEFORE the auction.
7. Don't think in terms of getting a good result by negotiating after the auction – do everything in your power to get the property on the market before the property gets passed in.
8. Get your client to be prepared to drop the Reserve Price if they have to.
9. Always discuss a Vendor Bid with your client or with the auctioneer – make sure the auctioneer can declare the property on the market on the very next bid.

Chapter 8:
Auction Day

This is the day you have been working hard towards for the last four weeks, no turning back, this is it! I can tell you now I don't care how seasoned a salesperson you are or how many auctions you have conducted, you will get nervous on the build up to this moment – that is if you really care about your clients and your work. But remember this: no matter how nervous you are your clients will be ten times worse and it is your job to keep them calm and reassure them all the way through. Now by reassure, I don't mean build up false hopes or unrealistic expectations. When I have an auction listing on the day we set the reserve price I tell the owners every possible scenario with what could happen at the auction so that we are all on the same page and we have back up plans in place should we need them. I always say to my clients:

"What's the worst possible thing that can happen? You don't sell. This doesn't mean you won't sell, you will probably be sold within three weeks of the auction (and I have to say, this seems to be spot on with the time), *you just didn't get a result under the hammer. It's not the end of the World! However, if you get a good chance to get the hammer down on the day, go for it! You will have an unconditionally sold property,*

no further waiting, no valuation issues, no pest & building report issues – job done!"

The common sense of this statement rarely fails. Now, let's move on to what actually happens on the day of the Auction:

If you are holding the auction on site there will usually be an open house immediately prior to the auction starting. If you have a group of auctions that are being held in rooms, this will normally occur on a week night – often a Thursday night, at a particular venue.

With on-site auctions when the property is marketed there will be a time as well as a date that the auction will commence. With in-rooms auctions there will be a venue and a general time advertised, but the Order of Sale for the properties is usually not available before that evening.

On site Auctions are normally started promptly at the time advertised, although there could be a delay for whatever reason. A buyer may be stuck in traffic and phone ahead and request that the Auctioneer delay proceedings and wait for them, or even the Auctioneer may be running late if they too get caught in traffic and are running between auctions. Whatever the reasons, there could be a delay, but usually that would only be for a few minutes.

In rooms Auctions, however, will usually start very promptly. If there are several properties on the Auction block on the same night, the Auctioneer must be very conscious of the time to get through all the stock. I have called over twenty auctions in one night, and, as the proceedings started at 7 pm and the hall closed at 11.30 pm promptly, I had to make sure I got through all the stock very efficiently.

When creating an Order for Sale for in-room auctions, you should select the most popular properties to begin the evening and to end the evening. The preferable order is to have the first three properties to sell to set the mood for the evening, then in the middle have the least popular and then keep the absolutely most popular property for the last auction. We want to keep the crowd in the room!

With in-room auctions there is usually a video played of each house prior to the auctioneer making reference to the contract and commencing the auction. I have attended many in-room auctions where buyers that have missed out on a previous property start bidding on a property just from these videos! In fact I have sold literally dozens of properties in-rooms sight unseen. It's amusing that when buyers get in the mood to buy, they will do this!

I have also had many on-site auctions where a buyer has turned up on the day of the auction, never seen the house before, and has registered, bid and won the property. Obviously to do this they must be financially well prepared and have a great deal of confidence in the market place.

I have never had a buyer walk into my office and buy a Private Treaty property without seeing it first! *NEVER!*

The following rules apply to New South Wales only:

Registering to Bid
First of all if anyone wishes to bid at an Auction in NSW, they need to register and to do this they need to have i.d. that will show their current place of residence and a photo of themselves. If they are electing to have someone else bid for them, both names, their i.d. and the i.d. of the person bidding for them need to be registered. They also have to give the Auctioneer an Authority that this person is bidding on their behalf. The ideal i.d. is a current Drivers Licence. If the buyer doesn't have one, then a utility bill with their name and current address plus some form of photo i.d. is acceptable – maybe a club membership card, or passport. Here in NSW if you do not hold a Drivers Licence you may obtain a voluntary Photocard to prove your identity. These are available from the Roads & Maritime Services at the local RTA office.

If the buyers are purchasing with partners such as a spouse, parent, sibling etc. then only one of them needs to register, not all parties. However all parties do need to sign the contract if they are the successful bidders.

Just remember, buyers do not have to bid just because they have registered, but a buyer certainly cannot bid if they are not registered! Auctioneers can be fined thousands of dollars if they accept a bid from an unregistered bidder! We don't make this mistake, I can assure you!

Once registered, the buyer must be given a number. This number is exclusive to them and must be shown every time they make their bid. Every Auctioneer in NSW today has an assistant recording each bid – it is a legal requirement. The bids are recorded by writing down the number of the bidder and the amount he has bid.

Before the start of the auction you have listed go over to your vendor and tell him how many buyers have registered to bid on your property. This may give him some indication of what to then expect. It will either make him more hopeful or it will ease him into seeing that a result may be hard to get. He will be less shocked with the outcome and therefore less stressed. It is your job to hold his hand. The more bidders the better, but don't be disappointed if it's less than you were expecting – you may still get a terrific result.

Auction Warning Signs

Before the start of the Auction, whether on site or in rooms, the Auction Warning Signs must be on display. In some States, they need to be on display for a specific amount of time, depending on the State's bye laws governing auction.

Some Auctioneers read out these rules, some don't. Personally, I do and the reason I do this is because I know I work in an area where English is the second language to most people, and even though they may be fluent in speaking English this does not necessarily mean they can read English.

I will now go through rules that apply in NSW individually with an explanation for each point:

1. **The Auctioneer must have the Reserve Price in writing prior to the commencement of the Auction.**

This is self-explanatory. If I don't have this, I don't call an Auction. I have had owners tell me on several occasions to "just call the Auction – I'll let you know if I'm selling". No, sorry, no can do. I am not risking my licence on an instruction that is contrary to the law. And you, as the agent, should have attended to this well prior to the Auction.

The reserve price that the owner sets can move down during an Auction, but never up. From an Auctioneer's point of view I prefer a realistic Reserve

Price which is gauged from buyer feedback during the Auction campaign. However, many owners like to inflate the reserve price so that they can make their final decision on what they will take as the Auction is actually being called. This may mean that I have to stop the Auction and consult with the Vendor if the bidding stops before the Reserve Price is reached.

2. **The Vendor is allowed one Vendor Bid only. If this bid is used the Auctioneer must announce in a clear and precise manner that this bid is on behalf of a Vendor.**

Personally I don't like using a Vendor Bid because this is usually the death knell of an Auction, but on occasions I will use it, provided that I can also state that the next bid will be the buying bid. That is up to the Vendor. I will discuss the use of a Vendor Bid prior to the Auction and I will usually set this with each Vendor as a fall-back position if I need to use it.

3. **The highest bidder is deemed to be the purchaser, subject to the reserve price.**

Again, self- explanatory. If the property is "On the market" this means that the reserve price has been reached and if the bidding stops at any point thereafter the property is sold.

4. **In the event of a disputed bid, the auctioneer is the sole arbitrator and the auctioneer's decision shall be final.**

If one person claims a bid was theirs and that is contrary to the bids recorded I have the authority to declare who the bid was taken from. No-one can argue with this. I can also refuse to accept a bid which I deem is not in the best interest of the Vendor. What does this mean? Well, if a bidder appears to be intoxicated I will not take his bid.

Also, I can set the pace of the Auction by refusing small bids that are far away from market value or the reserve price. For example: if a property has a reserve price of $600,000 and a bidder opens at $400,000, I will then call for a bid of say $420,000 or $450,000 immediately after. If someone bids $401,000, I can refuse that. I will set the increments that I wish to raise the bidding. You as the agent can give your instructions to the auctioneer prior to the start of the Auction. If your client has set a ridiculously high reserve price but will probably put the property on the market at a much lower figure, let this be your guide.

5. **A bidder is taken to be a principal unless before bidding the bidder has given to the auctioneer a copy of a written authority to bid for or on behalf of another person.**

Should the buyer bring someone to the Auction to bid on their behalf all parties have to be registered, the bidder has to be nominated and the auctioneer has to be given an authority in writing from the buyer that they want this person to bid for them.

If the buyer cannot attend the Auction on Auction day they can still bid by telephone. To do this they need to register (which can be done any time prior to the Auction date) and they can nominate a real estate agent or friend to bid on their behalf with themselves on the other end of the phone giving instructions. Again, the nominated bidder will also have to register, but it will still be the buyer signing the contract. Arrangements will have to be made with the owner's permission, as to when the contract can be signed.

6. **A bid cannot be accepted after the fall of the hammer.**

An Auctioneer can be fined several thousands of dollars if they accept a bid once the hammer comes down. I often have bidders trying to play cat and mouse with me – why, I'll never know! But they leave it right up until I am at the third and final call before they make their move. Although I do draw out waiting for a buyer, I cannot let that be for too long. I never bring the hammer down quickly, but I cannot give preferential treatment to a bidder that is agonisingly slow in making a decision.

7. **As soon as practicable, after the fall of the hammer, the purchaser is to sign the agreement for sale.**

The successful bidder is escorted to a table to then sign the contract and pay the agreed deposit. Regardless of how much information we agents give buyers, there will always be a rogue one that gets to this point and tells us that they are buying on behalf of their child/brother/uncle and that these people have to sign the contract, not the bidder. Not acceptable. Whoever registered to bid has to sign the contract. They can put "or Nominee" on the contract and if that leaves them liable to pay extra Stamp Duties, that's their bad luck. Otherwise this contract is invalid and should the buyers change their mind, there is no penalty and you are left with a house unsold.

Should this occur and the buyer refuses to sign the contract but wants you to wait until the relative turns up, refuse to do so. Refuse to sell them the property and to go to the under bidder and take his offer. Otherwise your client is extremely vulnerable right up until the point of settlement.

At every Auction I call I also announce the deposit rule, which is:

Unless before bidding the bidder has been granted a request by the vendor to place less than 10% deposit on the day, the vendor can refuse to sell the bidder the property.

Although I have already dealt with this, I will go over it again:
The successful bidder's options to pay the deposit are either by personal cheque, bank cheque or Deposit

Guarantee Bond. I have had bidders turn up to Auctions with plastic bags full of cash, I have to say, but in this day and age I would refuse to accept large sums of cash – it leaves us way too vulnerable to theft. Most agencies are only insured for a limited amount of cash stolen (approximately $2,000 per day) so if we take possession of tens of thousands of dollars, we are liable and responsible for that money until it is banked! One agent I know had a deposit of $80,000 stolen from the person doing the banking in the middle of the High Street in the middle of the day! And he had to cover this loss himself!!

The other disadvantage of taking wads of cash are that we then have to sit and count it – not a time friendly activity if we are calling another Auction straight after this one!

What I do want to emphasise however, is that if several requests are made of you prior to the start of the auction to exchange on a lesser figure than 10%, I would advise you to do so, otherwise you are eliminating bidders. The more bidders eligible to bid, the better the result should be and that is in your client's favour, not the buyer's.

The Actual Auction
So the time has come for the actual auction to commence. What should you expect? First of all I suggest you position your client in a place that is discreetly out of the way so that he can witness all the

proceedings and yet still be very accessible if you or the auctioneer needs to seek his instructions. I also suggest that where you position the vendor is separate from the bidders so that any conversations you may have remain confidential.

Obviously all auctioneers have their own methodology, but generally speaking they will call the crowd to order and welcome them to the property. With In-rooms auctions they will play the videos of the property. They may read out the terms of purchasing at auction and they will then refer to your Contract for Sale and read out general information such as settlement time (standard is 42 days from exchange to settlement), inclusions in the sale (i.e. dishwasher, clothes line, TV antenna etc.)

Once these formalities are over, the auctioneer will then call for an opening bid. I am going to deal with the actual bidding process later, but there are a couple of things I wish to tidy up now. There are basically two differing styles of auctioning. They are the English Auction, or open ascending price auction (which is the most popular style these days) and the Dutch Auction or open descending price auction. The difference between these two styles is that with the English Auction the bidding starts low and is worked upwards by the Auctioneer and with the Dutch Auction the Auctioneer calls out high figures and then drops these down until someone starts to bid. I much prefer the English Auction and work from low to high.

I don't like the other method at all. When I call an auction I am not concerned at how low the bidding starts, I am looking for participation more than anything else, and then setting the tempo of the bidding.

Tips from this chapter:

1. On site auctions will commence straight after the last open house; In-rooms auctions will take place at a nominated venue, usually on a week night.
2. With an on-site auction position your client so that you and/or auctioneer can access him to gain his instructions if necessary. Choose a location that is convenient for this but also positions him to observe all the activities.
3. With In-rooms auctions the order of sale should have the best properties positioned at the beginning and at the end. Keep the crowd in the room!
4. Buyers can emerge from the crowd and can bid, buy and surprise everyone – this will only happen with an auction listing.

5. All buyers must be registered before they can bid, and they must hold up their unique number so that their bids can be recorded.
6. The Auction Warning Signs must be on display prior to the start of the auction. Some auctioneers will read them out, but not always.
7. These Bye Laws must be adhered to or they can jeopardise the sale. Agents and auctioneers can be heavily fined if they do not follow the rules.
8. Explain how important it is to be very reasonable with the amount of deposit or settlement times (if possible) to allow as many bidders to participate in the auction as possible.
9. Don't allow the successful bidder to then try to arrange for an absent party to buy the property if they haven't observed the rules and done all the necessary registering that they needed to do – this could mean that the exchange is invalid and the buyers can pull out right up until the day of settlement without losing their deposit!
10. If your Auctioneer is using the English Auction method – that is starting low and rising with each bid, do not be alarmed if the bidding starts off low. Your auctioneer just needs participation at the beginning of the auction and to then set the tempo of the auction. This is vital.

Chapter 9:
The Bidding

This is probably the most important aspect of an auction and the most difficult to determine. Every single auction I have called (and that's probably hitting the thousands now) is completely unique. However, I shall try to capture as much information as I can for you so that you will see all scenarios and nothing will surprise you on the day.

First of all I want to say this: The absolutely worst thing that can happen is that the house doesn't sell under the hammer. **THIS IS NOT THE END OF THE WORLD!** I have seen owners and agents get so psyched up over an auction that they are almost sick with worry until the whole thing is over. Regardless of the need to sell, **CHILL!** Provided that your client's have listened to your advice, haven't moved the goal-posts, and have set a sensible reserve price, there is every chance the property will sell. If it doesn't sell at the actual auction, then take heart in the fact that most properties that don't sell under the hammer will probably sell within three weeks of the auction.

No Registered Bidders
First of all, if there are no registered bidders, there is no auction. Many owners (and agents) are

devastated by this, but it can happen. If this happens to you there really needs to be a meeting with you and the client to work out why this happened. Have there been changes in the marketplace? Did the auction date conflict with a long weekend or a sporting event? Was too high an opening bid put on your property? Is this property unusual or in a difficult location that put buyers off? Set a date to have this meeting but not immediately after the auction. Make sure you give yourself enough time to contact the parties that had expressed interest that were a no show and get their feedback as to why they didn't attend. Then put a sensible price on the property and start advertising it as a Private Treaty sale. You will get a result.

Registered Bidders but No Bids

Regardless of the methodology of the auctioneer (i.e. whether he uses the English Auction or the Dutch Auction), there needs to be a starting bid from a registered bidder to kick the whole thing off. Occasionally an agent will have advertised an "opening bid..." or "bidding starting from..." and that figure will be called out by the auctioneer. Most auctions do not have opening bids and the auctioneer has to wait for a figure to be called from the bidders. The majority of auctions start with deathly silence as the Auctioneer is calling for that first bid and waits for the crowd's response. And they wait. And they wait. And they wait.

Now occasionally we have auctions that do have attendees that register, yet still no-one bids and the property has to be passed in. Passing a property in with no bids is preferable to passing it in with a very low bid recorded. The reason I say this is because when we market the property after the auction, enquiring buyers will often ask "What was the property passed in at?" A low figure could influence their thinking and perception of its value.

Registered Bidders that Bid
So eventually the auctioneer has coaxed a bid out of the bidders and the auction slowly starts. I can honestly say that at the beginning of an auction, I really don't care how low the buyers start the bidding – all I am looking for at this stage is the participation so I can get the whole thing to roll along. Just remember that the bidders are probably even more nervous than you at this time. Not many of us want to draw attention to ourselves and bidding at an auction can be very intimidating.

Auctioneers will steer an auction by suggesting the increments they want from the bidders. So if the bidding starts really low, I may be calling for the next bid to be $50,000 or $20,000 more. Once I get close to reserve I shall then look at taking lower increments, maybe $10,000 or $5,000 bids. When I get within $20,000 of reserve, I could then be calling for bids of $2,000 or $1,000 – sometimes even $500 bids, depending on the strength of the bidders. My job is to get to reserve price, whatever that may be. I will not make a judgement call on market value of the property – that is not my responsibility. However I will be guided by you the agent. Once I reach that reserve figure, I will then allow virtually anything, but I have never been an Auctioneer that will allow increments of under $500. We are selling property, not cattle!

Once the tempo is established the bidding can be relatively swift, but not always. There may be several contenders at the beginning, but eventually this could fade to just two or three bidders. Seasoned bidders, if they really want the property, will throw in strong bids - $10,000, $20,000 etc. to put their opponents off. And other seasoned bidders may respond back with just $1,000 bid to show they are not put off. Each bid will be acknowledged by the auctioneer and recorded by their assistant. It is your job, as the listing agent, to walk around the bidders and encourage them to put in their bids. By encourage them *I DO NOT MEAN PUT PRESSURE ON THEM!* Don't be that kind of agent, please. Simply walk up and encourage, then move around to the other bidders. Good floor work from a lister is a great way to get another listing from someone in the crowd observing. If you just stand there and let the auctioneer do all the work, you are not doing your job.

If the Reserve Price is reached

Once the reserve price is reached, declaring the property "On the Market!" is at the discretion of the auctioneer. What I normally do, if we have sailed past the reserve price, is wait until the bidding has slowed down before I make this declaration. I don't want people to be put off bidding – I want the competition to gather momentum. But when it does slow down I will say *"It's on the Market! I am selling today! Make no mistake, if there is no further bidding I'm bringing the hammer down on this one and it will be SOLD!"* Often this fires up the bidding again, but the bids are usually small at this stage, although I have seen buyers throw in big bids to knock out the competition, and that often works. What can also happen is that new contenders start to bid once they know they can now buy the property. I have had many auctions where the actual buying bids are made by buyers that haven't made a bid until the property is well and truly on the market and I am just about to bring the hammer down.

After the bidding has completely finished and under-bidders are shaking their heads that they no longer wish to continue bidding, I will "Call" three times and then finally say "Are you all silent? Are you all done? Then this property is SOLD!" I have to be very careful at this stage, and I do take my time, because once the gavel (hammer) hits the table, board, or newspaper that I may be holding, I cannot take another bid. If an auctioneer does he can be heavily fined! So if there are any late bidders they could miss out – more importantly, the owner could miss out on more money! An auctioneer's job is to sell the property for as much money as he can get for the owner – so I don't bring the hammer down quickly. I want to get the juice out of the buyers for all my owners! Now you, as the agent, can tell me, the auctioneer, to wait a minute whilst you go around all the bidders to make sure that no-one wants to make another bid. If you instruct me to wait, I am more than happy to do this. This is your listing, not mine, it is you that must ensure your vendor has gotten the best possible price.

After the hammer comes down and the brouhaha has calmed down, the buyers are then invited to sign the contract and pay the agreed deposit.

What happens if the Reserve Price isn't reached?
Ok, so in the above scenario, the property is sold, however, if the bidding stops before the Auctioneer declares that the property is "On the market …" it means that the bidding hasn't reached the reserve price. What will normally happen then is that the agent and or Auctioneer will consult the owner to see what he want to do. If he is willing to drop his reserve price to this last bid figure to sell, and instructs the Auctioneer to do this, the Auctioneer will declare that the property is "On the Market!" Sometimes this may then kick the bidding on and other contenders may start bidding again. Otherwise the Auctioneer has permission to sell at this last bid price.

The agent or the Auctioneer should do their utmost to bring the last bidder and the owner together before the fall of the hammer. So there could be a lot of work by the agent or the Auctioneer, going back and forth between the last bidder and the owner, and this is why I suggest that the owner should be accessible, but out of earshot of the bidders. At this point the owner has to make a crucial decision. If he refuses to accept the last bid or offer, the property will be passed in and all negotiations will be done with the last person to bid only. This then eliminates the rest of the field. I can rattle off heaps of examples where owners have bitten the bullet, put the property on the market, and then sold at a great price, so make sure your owner thoroughly understands this.

If an agreement is made between both parties, the Auctioneer will state that "the buyer has increased his offer to …… and the property is now on the market, I am selling today!" This doesn't mean that the property has sold, because anyone else can now throw in a bid, and often they do.

But if the owner is not willing to sell at the price the bidding has stopped at and the buyer will not increase his offer to a figure acceptable to him, the Auctioneer will state that if there are no further bids he will "Pass In" the property. When this happens, then the last bidder has the first right to negotiate after the Auction and that buyer will still buy under Auction conditions, which means he signs the contract, pays the agreed deposit and the property is sold unconditionally.

If no agreement can be made with this bidder, the agent will then approach any of the other under-bidders to see if they are willing to pay a figure that the owner will take. Don't think for one minute that negotiating after the auction is stronger than negotiating before the auction finishes. All the pressure is on the buyer before the property is passed in to him. Afterwards, he is more likely to feel that he is in the driving position. And don't forget, passing in a property eliminates the rest of the field. I know it seems strange that buyers will continue to bid or start to participate in bidding only if the property is on the market, but in actuality, this happens all the time.

If the bidding has stopped way under the reserve price, for whatever reason, or if there is only one person bidding on the property, then the auctioneer may use the Vendor Bid. This should be discussed well prior to the auction, usually when you are setting the reserve price. Like I advised before, the best way for the Vendor Bid to act as a trigger is to allow the auctioneer to announce that the next bid will be the buying bid, so set this Vendor Bid accordingly.

The property can sell under auction conditions with a registered bidder up until 12 midnight of the day of the auction. If an unregistered bidder wants to buy during this period and none of the registered bidders are interested, then you can sell the property, but under cooling-off conditions only.

If there is no chance of an immediate sale, then you will have to put an asking price on the property and proceed to market as a Private Treaty listing. Should this occur, don't despair! You will probably make the sale within the next two or three weeks! The only thing that will stop this is if the owners have been and still are, far too rigid on the price they are expecting to sell for. Just remember you have had massive exposure of the property and there could well be buyers wanting but were not in a position to attend an auction.

Tips from this chapter:

1. It is not the end of the World if the property doesn't sell at auction! On average it will be sold within the next two to three weeks.
2. If there are no registered bidders there is no auction and it will be cancelled. Then arrange a meeting with your client so that you can analyse why this occurred and how you proceed from here. Same applies if there are registered bidders, but no-one bids.
3. Prepare your owner to drop the reserve price should the bidding stop before this is reached. A sale under the hammer is unconditional and the buyer is committed to the sale with a large deposit which he would have to forfeit to the owner should he change his mind after the auction. Also, auction conditions are "Buyer Beware!" there can be no further negotiations after an auction. This property is SOLD!

Chapter 10:
The End Result

So the hammer came down and the property successfully sold! Congratulations! Job well done! Now what happens?

The buyers should be ushered to a table to sign the contract whilst the rest of the field vacate the property – the show is over. With In-rooms auctions there is usually a side office where this is performed. The first job is to seal the deal by getting the contracts exchanged, and the quicker this is done the better.

The agent must write down the buyers' details on the front page of the contract together with their solicitor's details. They must also write in the sale price at the appropriate space on the front page of the contract and they must get the buyer to sign this document. If more than one party are buying the property then they all have to sign this document. If a Company is buying then a Company Director will have to sign this document. The deposit is then paid by whichever method and whatever amount has been agreed upon and the buyer will be issued with a receipt for that.

Once the buyer(s) have signed and paid that deposit, the owners will sign a second contract, if one is available. If for some reason there is only one document, all parties can sign this, although it is not desirable. But anything can happen at an auction. Sometimes a prospective buyer will ask to look at the contract prior to the auction and then inadvertently walk off with it in his pocket. I have to say this has never happened to me, but it can happen and if it does it throws a spanner in the works! So be prepared, you can exchange on one contract.

Once all parties have signed the documents and the deposit is paid both contracts are dated with that day's date. That is it. You have just sold a property! The agent should take both contracts with him, do his necessary paperwork and then send the owner's signed contract to the buyers' solicitor and their signed contract to the owner's solicitor. You should send letters to all parties straight after, congratulating your clients on the transaction and to confirm the amount of money you are holding.

Prior to settlement the buyers are entitled to conduct a final inspection. At that point they can walk through the property and look for any damage or any missing inclusions that may have happened or been taken after the exchange of the contract. They cannot argue about issues or damages that were like that at the time of the auction - that was up to them to notice - but anything afterwards should be addressed by the vendor.

The agent must accompany them on this inspection and act as witness to the proceedings. Also, the buyers should be able to expect any rubbish to be removed from the site by the owner. Most owners are very obliging and leave their home in immaculate condition, but occasionally we do get some minor issues that need to be addressed, and this can be done through solicitors at this time. Once this is done settlement will take place.

In most cases the agents are the stakeholders for the 10% deposit and this money is safely deposited into a Trust Account. This money can only be released prior to settlement for the purchase of another property and can only be paid into another Trust Account. Trust Account monies are not eligible for interest. Should both parties want this money invested until settlement, which can happen where there is a delay in settlement, then both the buyers and the sellers need to supply the agent with their Tax File Numbers. The standard time frame from exchange until settlement is usually 42 days. The acting solicitors will arrange between themselves the actual settlement date and they will inform you once this is established.

All the keys to access the property and remotes for garage doors, security gates etc. need to be with the agent prior to settlement unless other arrangements have been made between all parties. No keys should be handed out by the agent to the buyer before settlement takes place. Sometimes there can be a delay in the settlement for a variety of reasons and if settlement is postponed then the buyer should be denied access to the property unless this is specifically allowed by the owner. Agents cannot just assume a settlement has taken place just because it was scheduled for a specific day and time, they must check and make sure it has happened.

Once settlement has happened the agent needs to obtain Orders from both parties' solicitors. These Orders will then allow him to subtract his commission from the deposit he is holding in his Trust Account and then supply the owner with the balance of these funds. This can either be sent out by cheque or they can be electronically transferred into the client's account. Don't forget to obtain these instructions to make this happen, and this a great time to get a testimonial from a happy client.

Once more, Congratulations on the Sale of this Property! I hope you found this information useful.

Tips from this chapter:

1. Once the hammer comes down it is imperative that the contracts are signed and exchanged and the agreed deposit is paid according to either the contract or specific agreement.
2. The signed contracts must be sent out to respective solicitors the very next working day by the agent and written confirmation must be sent to all parties. Your clients can now start to pack!
3. The buyer will probably be advised to do a final inspection very close to the settlement date. This actual date will be organised by the respective solicitors.
4. The buyer is entitled to reimbursement for any damage done to the property after the auction, and is entitled to take possession of the property in a clean state with all rubbish removed. The agent will accompany the buyer for this inspection and act as a witness.
5. Once the agent receives the Orders from both solicitors he will then deduct his commission and forward the balance by either cheque or electronic transfer, to the vendor. Don't forget to obtain your client's instructions and this is a great time to get a testimonial!

Summary

What I would like to do now is summarize the benefits for all parties regarding the auction process, because I really do feel that this is a WIN-WIN-WIN situation for all parties, not agents exclusively nor vendors exclusively.

Why Buyers Should Love Auctions
In a rapidly moving market place like we are experiencing in Sydney at the moment, properties are getting snapped up the moment they hit the market. For example last Saturday I had three new properties come onto the market and all three sold immediately after the first respective open houses. This often means that buyers don't even have a chance of seeing fresh stock and if they do, they don't have time to give any thought to making a decision, they have to act straight away. With an Auction listing there is a four week programme which gives a buyer the opportunity to revisit the property several times, check out other properties to compare against it, get their finances organised and get reports done on the auction property.

If a snap decision has to be made on a property here in New South Wales, should the buyer change his mind about the property *FOR ANY REASON* he forfeits his initial .25% deposit. Now *FOR ANY REASON* can mean that the property is riddled with termites, has leaking showers which may have caused rotting subfloors, have leaking roofs etc. etc. With an auction property *NO MONEY CHANGES HANDS* unless or until a buyer has the hammer come down on his bid at an auction. Therefore there is no loss to the buyer except possibly for a pest report prior to an auction. I have had buyers come to me that have lost initial deposits two, three and four times! Working that out, that is a loss of possibly in excess of $5,000 – which eats into their deposit monies – through no fault of their own. If a buyer wants to get these reports done before he signs a contract he may find that by the time the reports are back someone else has snapped up the property, so he really is in a Catch 22 situation.

We do see some cash buyers around, but I would suggest that possibly 95% of buyers in our area need to borrow money from either a bank or some kind of lending body to purchase a home. So the buyer is vulnerable to a Property Valuer's assessment of the value of the home and if that Valuation comes in too low then the buyer's loan is rejected. Now in a moving marketplace we occasionally get Valuer's that are either overly cautious themselves or are given criteria from the lending body to look at **SETTLED** sales rather than **UNCONDITIONALLY EXCHANGED** sales. If those comparable sales are six or more months old they will not reflect the value of the day. So the buyer then loses the property and his initial deposit.

And finally it is usual that the most motivated owners take their properties to auction and want a result as much as the buyer wants to buy, so there is a chance that at an auction you will get the property at its best price, depending on the competition on the day. And once that hammer comes down that's it, the property is SOLD. Sometimes we see a willing buyer who, for a whole series of reasons, cannot get an unconditional loan approval from his lending body within the cooling off period with a Private Treaty sale. He will then need to get an extension to that cool off, the vendor has changed his mind for any reason and will not sanction this, so not only does the buyer lose the property, but he also loses his deposit, or he takes a massive risk and puts down the ten percent deposit, which he has to forfeit if he cannot get finance! Not a financially healthy position for a buyer to be in.

These points must be pointed out to the buyer by us agents as soon as we hear "I don't like auctions!" Often it is lack of knowledge and understanding on the buyer's part rather than a bad experience that elicits this response. Now you can counter that.

Why Owners Should Love Auctions
Any owner selling for any reason should be given the option to take their property to auction. Current marketplaces are very rare and short-lived so the conditions right now are ideal for auction. However, even in a down turning market or a flat market, auctions are ideal. Why? Because they are based on a time frame which can act as leverage to make a buyer take action. And if you want your property sold having it on the market for months totally ruins its value. Buyers are savvier today than ever before and they study the market a lot closer. If they see a property on the market for a long time the first thing they ask themselves is "What's wrong with it?" and the offers they usually place on a property are much lower than the initial price that we agents expected the property to sell for in the early stages. Also, if a property stays on the market too long the owners are more inclined to let it

Summary

go at a low figure just to get the job done. Not a good way to sell.

As far as pricing a property is concerned, like I say all the time, there is no scientific formula to assess its value. There can be strong comparables, true, but so often there are so many emotional reasons someone buys a particular property that this is hard to discern at the point of listing. The ideal regarding the auction is that the marketing is not based on a price, but on the property itself. There may be price guidelines placed in the advertising, but that is all they are – guidelines. There are other factors that just cannot be determined, such as proximity to local amenities or family members that are completely unique to that property. Or the presentation of the property. There are so many variables!

And in a rapidly rising marketplace why shouldn't an owner maximise his return from an asset that he has worked so hard to own? He is taking a risk with an auction in that he is paying up front fees for the marketing etc. but by doing this he is going to see competitive bidding which he can only benefit from.

Also, with a Private Treaty sale, the owner is in the worst possible position. A buyer may make a rapid decision and a good offer on the property, but can just as easily withdraw that offer and that leaves the owner having to go right back to the beginning of the process again. Should this happen twice or three times then other buyers can believe there is something wrong with the property, which may not be the case, and the offers will start coming in lower. If the owner needs a quick sale, this again will leave him no choice but to accept that lesser figure.

The control of the sale is more with the owner under auction conditions regarding settlement time, inclusions etc. Not so with a Private Treaty sale. And finally, there can sometimes be that little bit of magic that happens at auction and nowhere else. The buyers that turn up out of the blue and bid to the max! Wonderful ... and only at auction.

Why Agents Should Love Auction
Need I really spell this out for you? Seriously? Ok then, if you insist!

First of all, when an owner has invested his own money into the sale of a property it signifies that he is highly motivated to sell. How many vendors have you worked hard for that have really been half-hearted about selling and you have run yourself ragged for them? Yes, we are a "service industry" and part of that service is to work for clients who may eventually not sell, and handled properly they will come back when they are well and truly ready. But I do not want a whole collection of these types of vendors! I am in this profession to earn a living after all.

What I particularly like about auctions is that all the work is done at the forefront. Marketing strategies are super important, open houses, inspections etc. we do all this for any listing, but auctions really do keep you on your toes with the frequency of the feedback and the quality of the feedback that you give your owners. Once you are doing this for auction properties you set a higher standard for all your stock. One of the biggest complaints against real estate agents is that we don't keep in touch with our clients often enough. We seem to chase them no end to get the listing and once we have it we don't ring half as often!!!

I believe that the most important part of looking after a listing is educating our vendors. We need to educate them to the thoughts of the buyers, which may not synchronise with what we originally told our vendors. Realistically we can only really price a property once we start taking people through that are in a position to buy it. They see all the stock on the market and have a far broader picture of what is available and what is competing with our stock at that given time. So getting their opinion of value is crucial to our vendors, yet so many agents are terrified of telling their owners this truth. Disassociate yourself from this and give the owner this feedback! This feedback is not the same as submitting an offer. Buyers may have an opinion of a property's value, but may not be willing to buy even at the price they think it's worth, there is a difference. But it is this opinion that is vital information that your vendor needs to know. And giving owners written reports is crucial. There is a vast difference in communication between a conversation over a telephone and the written word. A telephone conversation can be half listened to, misinterpreted, or forgotten. The written word is there in front of them, nothing disguised by them or you and cannot be avoided.

But what I absolutely love about auctions and always will, is that if I choreograph the sale properly, supply the correct uncompromising information, set the reserve price with a well thought out strategy, the hammer comes down on the day and it is a sealed deal! With private treaty sales a salesman's (and owner's!) heart is in his mouth until that 10% deposit goes down and anything can happen up until that point. I don't want my owners to be threatened or held to ransom at the eleventh hour by a ruthless purchaser/purchaser's solicitor. Or to find out that finance isn't approved, a bathroom leaks, the buyer's found a better deal etc. etc. etc. Nor do I want to have to renegotiate a price or terms otherwise the deal falls through. And regardless of the state of the market if a property comes back on the market for whatever reason, there is not the same momentum as there was when it first came on.

To me an Auction Listing means a SALE!

GLOSSARY OF TERMS

Agent.

The person acting on behalf of the vendor

Agreement for Sale

Or Contract for Sale. The legal document usually prepared by a legal advisor (solicitor or conveyancer) which must be available before a property can be marketed

Auction

A public sale in which goods or property are sold to the highest bidder

Auctioneer

A person who conducts auctions by accepting bids and declaring goods sold

Bidder

Any person registered to bid at an Auction

Buyer Beware

The Golden Rule of Auction which puts the responsibility on the buyer that if he purchases at Auction, he buys "as is"

Caveat Emptor

The Latin version of above

Deceased Estate

The owner of the property has died and the property is being sold by either the beneficiaries or the Public Trustee

Dutch Auction or open descending price auction

The auctioneer calls for high bids and then drops and drops until a bid is made

English Auction or open ascending price auction – currently the most

popular form of auction.

The Auctioneer begins from a low opening bid and brings the bidding up in increments determined by him/her to the reserve price and possibly beyond

Fall of the Hammer Or hammer comes down.

When the Auctioneer hits the gavel on the table, or anything else, which indicates that the property is sold

On the Market

The reserve price has been reached and the Auctioneer has the authority to sell the property to the highest bidder

Open House

An allotted time, usually on a Saturday, when the property is open to the Public to inspect without an appointment

Opening Bid

An indication of where bidding will start for a property. This is usually 10-20% under the anticipated reserve price or the owner's ideal sale price

Mortgagee in Possession

When the lending body has taken possession from an owner for non-payment of their mortgage

Passed In

The reserve price hasn't been reached and the owner refuses to sell at the last bid price

Reserve Price

Usually the least amount the Vendor is willing to take at Auction to allow a sale to ensue. This must be given to the Auctioneer in writing before the start of the Auction

Registration

It is law in NSW today that all bidders must be registered and to do this they must show photographic id with their Current address to the selling agent, who will then recordthese details and issue that person with a unique number   which must be shown as a bid is made.

Auctioneers can be heavily fined if they take a bid from an unregistered bidder, however this bid is still deemed to be valid

Vendor Bid

A bid made by the Auctioneer on behalf of the Vendor

About the Author

Maria Lawrance started her career in Real Estate in September 1986. She is a Licensed Real Estate Agent and an Accredited Auctioneer, and has won many awards in her career.

Back in 1989 Maria was the first woman in her then Franchise Group to win Salesperson of the Year and she had to beat 86 men to do it! It is an accolade she held for almost twenty years before another lady took that title. She also won Auction Lister of the Year in the same year, first person to ever do both !

Back in 1987 Maria participated in an Auction Listing training course and was one of the first people to introduce the Auction system to her area. Now she has literally thousands of auctions under her belt, both as an Auction lister and as a highly respected Auctioneer. She has Auctioned property all over

Sydney and has conducted both on site auctions and in-room auctions.

Maria sold the last of the three offices she owned in April 2011 with the intention of retiring. Len Pretti, a well known guru in Property Management, coaxed her to join his businesses. It didn't take much! Maria loves her work.

Even as a veteran of the real estate industry, Maria has some of the best results around. She has just sold her 100th property since joining Len's team two short years ago. Her conversion rate of listings to sales stands at 93%. But she is most proud of her statistic for Agent's opinion to sale price which currently stands at 99.83%! And her average time on market for those 100 sales is 5.2 weeks!

This year alone Maria has achieved some amazing results for property owners, with her best result being $600,000 over reserve price for one particular property!

She now wants to share her knowledge and her experience with the marketplace to leave a legacy in the industry she has proudly served for over 27 years.

There has never been a book written before to help sellers navigate through the Auction system. And with the useful tips and hints you will find in these pages, you should now be able to sell with confidence

"like" us on facebook

BUYING @ AUCTION

PROPERTY SUCCESS SERIES

TOP 10 TIPS TO SUCCESSFULLY BUY PROPERTY @ AUCTION

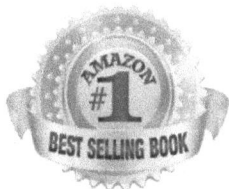

AMAZON
#1
BEST SELLING BOOK

LEADING AUSTRALIAN AUCTIONEER & AGENT
MARIA LAWRANCE

First Edition 2014 | Copyright 2014 by Maria Lawrance

ISBN-10:   0992416577
ISBN-13: 978-0-9924165-7-7

www.ingramcontent.com/pod-product-compliance
Lightning Source LLC
Chambersburg PA
CBHW072158270326
41930CB00011B/2476